LONDON
A SPIRITUAL HISTORY

"Edoardo Albert, son of Italian and Sri Lankan migrants, criss-crossed London for years to repair TVs. He relates the city's spiritual history: Christianity arriving from Italy, through King Alfred and the mediaeval church, taking in atheism and theosophy, up to Hillsong and the present. He relates his own spiritual history too, from Catholicism, through atheism, the occult and Islam, then back again. Both are intriguing. He reaches an important conclusion: 'London, seemingly without anyone noticing, has become over the last twenty years the most religious part of Britain churches are opening up all over the place.' And I think he's right."

— RT HON STEPHEN TIMMS, MP FOR EAST HAM

EDOARDO ALBERT

LONDON

A SPIRITUAL HISTORY

LION

Published by Lion Books
an imprint of
Lion Hudson plc
Wilkinson House, Jordan Hill Road,
Oxford OX2 8DR, England
www.lionhudson.com/lion

ISBN 978 0 7459 5696 1
e-ISBN 978 0 7459 5697 8

First edition 2016

Acknowledgments
pp. 34–35: 5 lines from *The Earliest English Poems* translated and introduced by Michael Alexander (Penguin Classics 1966, Third edition 1991) copyright © Michael Alexander, 1966, 1977, 1991. Used by permission.

p. 50: Extract from *Bede: Ecclesiastical History of the English People.* "The History" translated by Leo Sherley-Price and revised by R. E. Latham, translation of the minor works, new Introduction and Notes by D. H. Farmer (Penguin Classics 1955, Revised edition 1968, 1990). Translation copyright © Leo Shirley-Price, 1955, 1968. Introduction copyright © D. H. Farmer, 1990. Translation of "Bede's Letter to Egbert" and "Cuthbert's Letter on the Illness and Death of the Venerable Bede" copyright © D. H. Farmer, 1990. Used by permission.

pp. 145–146: *English Literature in the Sixteenth Century, Excluding Drama* by C. S. Lewis (1963, 1973). By permission of Oxford University Press.

p. 159: *Essays Presented to Charles Williams* by C. S. Lewis copyright © C. S. Lewis Pte. Ltd. 1966. Extracts reprinted by permission.

pp. 126, 131, 132: Extract from *Atheists: The Origin of the Species* by Nick Spencer. Copyright © Nick Spencer, 2014. Used by permission of Bloomsbury.

pp. 185–186: *The Silver Chair* by C. S. Lewis copyright © C. S. Lewis Pte. Ltd. 1953.

A catalogue record for this book is available from the British Library

Printed and bound in the UK, January 2016, LH26

For Harriet, Theo, Matthew, and Isaac

CONTENTS PAGE

ACKNOWLEDGMENTS

No book is produced alone, and this is no exception. I'd like to thank Alison Hull at Lion, for first giving me a chance there, and then piloting this book through some choppy waters to its final destination – as Stephen King once said, "To write is human, to edit is divine." And at Lion I'm blessed with a trio to match Paris's choice (but without the unfortunate consequences for Troy): not only Alison but also the two Jessicas, Tinker and Scott. Together, they have worked tirelessly to save me from my errors and infelicities. And when the book went for copy editing, I was most fortunate to have Drew Stanley running through the text with the greatest precision and a remarkable ability to remember contradictory things I'd written fifty pages earlier. Needless to say, whatever faults remain are mine, clung on to despite their advice to the contrary.

Writing might be a solitary profession, but for a writer to succeed, he needs support, and a family willing to put up with penury while he pursues his craft. My family has done so, and put up with the ups of elation and the downs of struggle that go with it, with quite heroic patience – I thank you (and put in a quick request for future forbearance too). So, Harriet, Theo, Matthew, and Isaac, this book is for you – you've earned it!

Links

Find out more about Edoardo Albert and his books and stories at www.edoardoalbert.com and on his blog: www.edoardoalbert.com/blog/. He would be delighted if you would like him on Facebook (he's there as Edoardo Albert as well) or follow him on Twitter @EdoardoAlbert (the advantage of an unusual name is that no one else has claimed it first).

BENEATH THE BELLY OF A WHALE

You can't do it now, but when I was a child you could walk under a whale. The model of *Balaenoptera musculus* (the blue whale) hung from the ceiling of the Natural History Museum. A skeleton hung alongside it, but it was the model that fascinated. Even now, as an adult, the size of the blue whale confounds me. Then, I was half as tall and it was at least ten times bigger, floating above me, its upcurving lips giving it an amused air, as if it was as surprised to find itself in the air as I was to see it there. That sealed it for me; the dinosaurs, the mammoths and sabre-tooth tigers, the giant deer and narwhal all drew me in, but it was the whale, Leviathan himself, that swallowed me. We became regular visitors to the museum, taking the tube from Holloway Road down to South Kensington and then the long, underground walk from the station to the museum entrance. It seemed an appropriately subterranean way to approach these creatures, dragged from earth and sea.

In memory, I wandered among wonders alone, in a museum devoid of crowds or crush. When I tried to recreate the zoological pilgrimages of my childhood with my own sons, we were driven from the museum by the unbearable press of people. Can the number of visitors have really risen so much, or does my memory impose the solipsism of childhood on its recollection of the museum?

You see, here's the deal. I was a child, the eldest son of immigrants. What, for them, was a strange, new world was home to me. What's more, I was the eldest son of Italian (my mother) and Sri Lankan (my father) immigrants. To complicate matters, my father was half Sinhala and half Tamil: his own parents had been disowned as a result of their marriage. I was a boy who loved reading, clever, well behaved, who did well at school and received glowing school reports. I was, in fact, the Asian immigrant archetype: a swotty, well-presented (through all my years at school, I never once returned home with shirt untucked or tie undone) pupil upon whom the mantle of "future doctor" had already been placed by my proud parents. Every Asian/Italian immigrant in the seventies wanted their son to be a doctor and I loved science, scoring top marks in biology, physics, chemistry and, with a little more effort, maths. What else was I going to be?

But God bugged me.

I don't remember the answer, but I remember the question. I was about six at the time.

"Mummy," I asked, "it says in the Bible that God created everything, but scientists say that animals evolved from other animals. Which is right?"

It was a trick question. I had a faith, and it was absolute. I believed in books. The most enjoyable trips of my childhood were to the library, where I would withdraw my allocated four books, or eight if it was a bank holiday, when you were allowed two books per ticket. Then, upon arriving home, came the delicious book-choosing ritual, when I decided in what order I would read my haul of wonders. Books contained worlds, books contained knowledge, books contained everything. And, since I read and my parents didn't, I concluded I knew more than they did.

I already knew the answer to my question. My biblical knowledge had come through church and the stories of my parents; but I had read – in books! – what scientists thought. Therefore they must be right.

So I became an atheist at the age of six (thus beating Christopher Hitchens in the childhood atheism stakes, as he only abandoned his belief in God at the relatively advanced age of nine). After all, I was the clever one, the one who read books; I knew stuff.

Oh, the power that thrilled my little frame. I had brought the heavens down and they had not broken me. What was more, I realized in the subsequent weeks and months that I had gifted myself an extraordinary bargaining chip. For now, when faced with losing three–nil in playground football or being stuck on the bus with the prospect of missing my favourite TV programme, all I had to do was say, "I don't believe in you, God, but if by any chance you do exist, then if you let us win the match/get home in time/insert as appropriate I will believe in you." As far as I remember, whenever challenged, my non-existent deity lived up to his part of the bargain. I, on the other hand, conscious of not losing my solitary bargaining chip, always reneged. I'd believe next time. This was the magical atheism of the child, akin to thinking myself invisible when I covered my eyes. The real death-of-God stuff awaited further disillusion.

Besides, I had other concerns. Most of all, I desperately wanted to fit in. This was 1960s London, Archway Road variety. Back then, Islington was a slum, Camden Town not much better, and the dearest wish of my parents was to be able to buy a semi-detached house in the suburbs. There just weren't that many foreigners around, and those that were, were mostly Irish and thus, to my eyes and ears, as English as the English. After all, they were all white, and Patrick sounded no less native than George. What definitely didn't sound native was "Edoardo", so I asked to be called "Eddie" because it sounded more like the names of the other boys and hearing it made me feel less the outsider. My teachers were in on the deal but, unfortunately, the headmaster at my first primary school, Mr Turrell, a remote but kindly man, was not made privy to the understanding. He continued to call me "Edoardo" to my humiliated, tearful despair. The problem was, I really was different. There weren't any other Italian/Sinhala/Tamil children at my school – and even if there had been, I wouldn't have wanted to have anything to do with them. I just wanted to belong. But, to the other children, I was a dago, a greaseball, a wop, an Eyetie, a paki – in fact, being a brown-skinned mixture meant that pretty well every racial stereotype could be used to describe me, bar nigger and sambo. Those were reserved for the black boys. But I had more!

However, this was no racist hell – the words were labels; they were rarely used with any intention to hurt, and I have no stories to tell of bullying or discrimination. But this language did serve to tell my brother and me that we were set apart, in our own group of two; there was no one else like us (I presume there must be someone out there with Italian/Sinhala/Tamil parentage, but if there is, I haven't met them). We were on our own.

Being on our own, mother took us wondering, and wandering, around the city. She had come to London at eighteen, unable to speak a word of English, but determined to learn. She had indeed learned, although her first employers (she worked as an au pair), taking advantage of her shyness and lack of language, virtually starved her. London was as strange and unknown to her as it was to us. There were no family memories of outings to recall, no reserves of her own childhood trips to draw upon; we had to discover the city together: one woman, and two small children (Father, of course, was out working during the week, and often at the weekends too).

Realizing she had bright and curious children, Mother took us to museums, with sandwiches prepared in the morning and carried along in paper bags. We visited them all, but the Natural History and Science museums were my favourite and, as senior brother and the more bookish, I prevailed in my insistence that we return often to South Kensington.

It was as rich a part of London then as it is now, but that plays no part in my memory. Only the animals figure, and the glorious halls of the museum, true cathedrals to my godless little mind. I had not mentioned my abjuration of faith to my parents. I had absorbed much of the spirit of the city, and its shrinking back from human involvement. I could decide for myself, without reference to anyone else, and that seemed so natural and obvious to me as to not even be up for consideration. This was something I could only have absorbed from my surroundings. You learn, as a child in the city, how to pass unnoticed and not draw attention to yourself. So I did within my own family, dutifully attending Mass, kneeling in silence before the altar, while all the time I had not even a smidgen of belief.

St Gabriel's, our parish church, was one of those churches erected in a sudden church-building rush in the 1960s to serve London's Irish immigrants – just up the Archway Road was the legendary Gresham Ballroom, where many a boy from Meath and a girl from Sligo met and matched.

In shape, St Gabriel's was an irregular polyhedron, in ecclesiology it was an uneasy mash-up of post-Vatican II enthusiasm, and in its interior it was bare dark-grey brick, relieved by eight or nine abstract stone ornaments stuck upon the wall in a pattern that, many Masses later, I can confidently assert was truly random. For human hands and eyes and mind, designed as we are to see pattern and symmetry and design, there is nothing harder to produce than something truly random, so I must congratulate the architect, Gerard Goalen – he did something very few others have done. He also managed to create the ugliest building it has ever been my misfortune to spend significant amounts of time in. St Gabriel's was not his only monstrosity – there are other brick boxes dotted around the country being mistaken for abattoirs. So, this dreary grey warehouse, with mothers and babies locked away in the crying room but looking like they were the only ones having any fun, this was the portal to heaven? Yeah, sure it was. I wasn't likely to believe that, not when we made regular pilgrimages to the Natural History Museum and I could see what a proper temple looked like, and soak in its atmosphere of quiet reverence. Indeed, has there been a church built in the last 150 years to match the Romanesque entrance and Great Hall of the Natural History Museum? I doubt it.

The architect of this wonder, although I paid him no thought at the time, was Alfred Waterhouse. But there would have been no museum at all without the vigorous politicking of Richard Owen, superintendent of the Natural History Department of the British Museum. For through the first three-quarters of the nineteenth century, natural, national, and international history were kept under the same roof in Bloomsbury, that roof belonging to the British Museum. Owen, a natural publicist, took Prime Minister William Gladstone around the crowded corridors of the museum in 1861, demonstrating how crammed the building was. By the end of the tour, Gladstone was convinced: natural history needed its own building. But where? "I love Bloomsbury much," said Owen, "but I love five acres more."

There were five acres, and more, on the site in South Kensington of the 1862 International Exhibition. The first plan was for the Natural History Museum to take over the buildings of the exhibition, but the parliamentary bill allowing it was defeated, and the exhibition buildings were torn down. Probably just as well: the building that housed the exhibition was widely disliked, its two crystal domes described as "colossal soup bowls" and *Art Journal* called the long, low building "a wretched shed". So it was somewhat surprising that the architect who designed the International Exhibition won the competition to build the Natural History Museum on the same site. That architect was Captain Francis Fowke, a Royal Engineer and the bearer of one of the most splendid Victorian moustaches ever to grace a philtrum. But before Fowke could begin work, he died suddenly of haemorrhage in 1865 and Alfred Waterhouse took over the plans for the nascent institution.

Fowke had planned a Renaissance-style building, and Waterhouse was bound to accept the overall design Fowke had bequeathed him. However, building work didn't begin until 1873 and the museum only opened in 1881, by which time Waterhouse had transformed Fowke's original winning design into the Victorian take on the Romanesque we see, its exterior clad in smog-resistant terracotta tiles. Waterhouse cleverly retained sufficient elements of Fowke's plan to persuade his supervisory committees that they had not had an entirely new design foisted upon them. One reason for the delay in starting work on the building may have been Richard Owen. Although widely respected as the leading authority on zoological and palaeontological classification of his day, he inspired deep and lifelong loathing in many. T. H. Huxley – Darwin's bulldog – wrote: "It is astonishing with what an intense feeling of hatred Owen is regarded by the majority of his contemporaries. The truth is, he is the superior of most, and does not conceal that he knows it."[1]

The dislike for Owen was deepened by the intellectual fault lines that opened up in Victorian society over Charles Darwin's theory of evolution. Owen opposed it – indeed, he is believed to have supplied Bishop Wilberforce with many of his arguments in the famous debate on evolution at Oxford between him, T. H. Huxley, and others – and thus earned the enmity of the theory's supporters. Nor did he have the social cachet of many of his foes, having come

---

1   Huxley, 1903, page 136.

from a poor, if middle-class, family. His relative poverty meant that he had to apprentice himself at sixteen to a surgeon apothecary rather than his family paying for him to attend medical school. This proved to be to Owen's immense advantage, however, as his duties included attending and assisting the post-mortems at Lancaster Gaol, thus enabling him to practise dissection frequently at a time when most medical students had to make do with one body a year. Owen became obsessed with anatomy and on one occasion, having acquired a dead black prisoner for dissection, he decided to take the head home for further examination. Unfortunately, he dropped it while making his way down a steep and slippery hill, and it bounded downwards, with the anatomist in hot pursuit. But the head, being better formed for rolling, made it to the bottom of the hill first, knocking to a stop against a front door. Owen, still running, arrived at the door just as it opened. Not surprisingly, the householder, confronted with a head lying at her door and an apparently mad man running towards her, departed screeching back inside. For his part, Owen wrapped the head in his cloak and beat a hasty retreat.

Being on the losing side in the great Victorian debate on evolution cost Owen much of his reputation, but his legacy endures in the building and institution he created. Although the vision was his originally, the building became the testament of Alfred Waterhouse.

The son of Quakers, Waterhouse was a devout man who converted to the Church of England later in life. In many ways, he was the perfect Victorian architect, able to work with committees and parsimonious budgets while maintaining good relations with just about everybody. But in common with much Victorian work, he fell out of favour in the twentieth-century dash to modernism and the self-conscious forgetting of the past. In fact, almost all the social history of Britain since the death of Queen Victoria can be read as a reaction against the Victorians: their achievements, from railways to biggest-ever empire via industrial revolution, so much greater than ours, and their failings, which we have magnified to escape that overbearing figure of maternal disappointment.

But while Waterhouse and Owen were both religious men, the museum opened when London had become the world's first megalopolis – the city by which the borning future would define itself. Waterhouse placed a statue of Adam on the apex of the parapet above the main entrance, to make the point that humanity was the pinnacle of creation. It's not there now. The statue survived until the Second World War, when it toppled from its plinth; rumours abound that Adam was pushed.

After all, the city was more real than its maker. This was the city that swallowed everything: goods, people, animals, life… God. This was the city that went on forever. It was a place through which a man could journey and feel "that now at last he must have come to the end of the universe, and then [find] he has only come to the beginning of Tufnell Park".[2] Peter Ackroyd, in *London: The Biography*, thinks the city pagan; and it is pagan in the sense that its gods are many. But in its pantheon three reign supreme: wealth and power have, throughout the city's history, danced an elaborate two-step, a pattern made physically manifest in the twin financial and political poles of the city, in the City and Westminster. And uniting them both, largely unspoken because never needing to be said, is the city itself, the unspoken idol of its masses, demanding sacrifice, unwitting though it is, and the most profound form of prayer, which is presence. For through almost all its history, London's death rate has exceeded its birth rate: the city could only grow by devouring the population of the rest of the country, and the rest of the world. People came, heads filled with dizzying dreams of fame, fortune, and freedom, and died. And yet the city kept growing, its belly fires consuming more people than any Moloch, its coffers

---

2   Chesterton, 1960, page 15.

swelled by their offerings in tax and commerce, and, most of all, its hunger for life assuaged by its votaries' presence. London is a dark god of a city, and I, unknown to myself, had fallen under its spell. There was nothing else but city, no sky above us (although the Tube was definitely below). Writers have sought restlessly a metaphor for London: Rome, Athens, Jerusalem even, but the city that sticks, the one that prefigures and mirrors it best, is Babylon. Babylon the Great, but Babylon has not fallen – it renews itself, again and again, growing carnivorously upon the body of Britain.

And yet... and yet... that is not the whole story of London. There is also the quiet of rain-washed streets, the excitement of stolen glances, the clash of ideas, and the deep peace, beyond the bustle and noise, of a city church and a city graveyard. People have found God in the city, as well as losing him there, as I did – casting faith aside in South Kensington and finding it once more in Bromley and Arnos Grove. Looking at the locations, I fear my faith may be suburban, but what of that? I will speak of the suburbs, the lost paradise of Betjeman's Metroland, now vanished beneath the red bricks of paved-over front gardens, sprouting ugly automotive growths. It is a long journey, and it has almost all taken place in the city.

London is where I must start, for the city, this deceiving, dreadful, delightful city, stole my faith from me when I was a child and it took many years and much searching to get it back.

So, first, I will travel through London the deceiver, the whore of the Thames, that dangles dreams and delights in front of you, the serpent city whispering in the ear, telling you that you can, indeed, have it all. Money, power, fame, sex, recognition, opportunity, freedom, anonymity. These are the significant siren songs of cities around the world, and London, as the first great city of the modern era, sings them louder than most. But Ackroyd is right – London is pagan rather than godless. It is too unruly, too unplanned, to be atheistic at its core. Paris, on the other hand, is a godless city, the divine, which is the mystery of love, banished by the geometrizing, clearing hand of Baron Haussmann. For God, who is mystery, to be recognizable in cities there must be corners, hidden alleys, lost squares which no one visits. A city laid out to geometrical patterns is the placing of human beings into a rationalist dream, the living embodiment of the observation that nineteenth- and twentieth-century atheism is an organic outgrowth of the rationalist theology of the seventeenth and eighteenth centuries. We thought our way to God, we built our dreams of him, and then found that he was no longer believable in such a milieu. The God we know too well is the God we cease to believe in.

London, as city, is both a metaphor and an illustration of our relationship with God. In this book, I will explore London's spiritual history, in its buildings and churches, its festivals and burnings. But the spirit meets matter in a life lived, and to that end, and with apologies for my presumption, I will interweave a personal narrative with the historical one. Although no life is typical of London – the city's inhabitants are too varied and their stories span every genre invented and some that have yet to be put to paper – yet I can still claim to have been born, of immigrants, here and to have lived my life within its boundaries. For many years I did a job that involved driving around London and visiting people in their homes – I was a TV repairman – so I got to understand the rhythms of the city and to see inside a huge cross section of people's homes and lives in a way that few others do. And the possibilities unleashed by the Reformation – possibilities ranging from killing off God to calling up spirits – were recapitulated in my own history. The city does not repeat stories, but it does have characteristic themes and, all unwittingly, those themes were played out in my life.

London: A Spiritual History takes its story from the city and its heart from the people who have lived and died, dreamed and prayed and despaired in its houses and on its streets. I hope you will accompany me through the centuries and along the many and varied byways of the spirit within the city.

PART I: OLD WAYS

CHAPTER 1

THE RIVER RUNS THROUGH IT

L ondon is made of itself. It is that it is. Let's take the Natural History Museum as an example. The substance of the building, its rich, red bricks, were fired from London clay – the museum, as with so much of London, was made out of its own depths, a recycling of material and ideas that has occurred throughout the city's history. London was an industrial city before any of the northern mill towns started production, the eastern and southern suburbs the location for the dirtier, smellier processes.

Among the key industrial processes was brick making, and here the makers had an advantage – they were standing on their raw material. London clay was ideal for London bricks. During the great Victorian expansion, builders stripped bare the fields that were to house the new suburbs, dug down to the layer of London clay beneath the topsoil, and fired it for bricks. Thus, the city was made from itself, its very substance first laid down in shallow seas, then filled over 25,000 years ago from the dust ground out by glaciers settling in the river basin of the Thames as they slowly retreated – a thought as pleasing as the knowledge that our physical bodies are stardust.

When the glaciers retreated again, some 10,000 years ago, the people arrived. Although these first Britons would certainly have been masters of boat building, crafting canoes and coracles from wood and skin, they didn't need the boats to get to the country, since it was, at the time, of one piece with the rest of Europe. But rivers were nevertheless important, as barriers, as pantries stuffed with good things to eat, as highways to travel along, and as a liminal zone where the human and the divine met, mingled, and left food and offerings out for each other. London, or the London area, was swiftly settled when people returned north.

The first, the very first, London was already double headed. The Thames, draining a vast area (16,000 square kilometres or 6,000 square miles) of southern England, flooded regularly and its banks were soft, marshy places, not the hard concrete confines we see today. Now, the river flows deep and narrow; then it was broad and shallow, with the transition from water to land much harder to define – think of a fenland landscape to try to get an idea of what it might have looked like. Today the river, running through its concrete channels, is some 1,000 feet or 300 metres from bank to bank. Then, unconfined, the waters ebbed and flowed in response to tide and rainfall, broadening to nearly a mile at high tide, shrinking to a few hundred yards at low. Where the City of London lies today, two small gravel hills emerged from the rushes and willows: Cornhill and Ludgate Hill. Flowing through the sedge between them was the Walbrook, which ran from its head near Finsbury or Shoreditch to join the Thames where Cannon Street station now is.

Given the river's propensity to flood, it made complete sense for the area's Palaeolithic and Neolithic visitors to set up camp on the area's higher, drier ground. For hunter gatherers, rivers and marsh were larder and store combined, the obvious fish and waterfowl supplemented by fibrous marsh plants, ideal for weaving and basketry, and seasonal tubers and roots.

But if they gathered, they also left, and often they left their best. Along the Thames, there is evidence of goods of great value, given to the river: objects of stone, copper, bronze, and iron made with care and wit and time. As with the extraordinary finds at Starr Carr, where a stilted walkway led out over the flat waters of the fen to allow offerings to be consigned to the depths, so there are signs that there were platforms built out over the Thames from which weapon or jewellery or vessel might be ritually broken and given to the river. Why broken, before being put into the water? Good question. The consensus among archaeologists appears to be that breaking was a sign of true giving – a broken sword could not be subsequently fished out and reforged. It belonged to the river, alone and forever.

So from the start, even before there was a city, the place of the city was marked by sacrifice. The river was a living, and demanding, god that required sacrifice that it might continue to bestow its beneficence upon its human visitors. The river, in truth, is older than the city, its father and begetter and, for most of the city's history, the channel of its connections with the country and world.

The power of the Thames is still visible today, although most Londoners never notice it. Stand on a bridge, or look out from the river's banks at the flowing dark water. Which way is it flowing? Out to sea, or upriver? Every six hours, the Thames reverses its direction as the moon pulls seawater inland and the river meets it with rainwater making for the sea. In fact, the Thames is so strongly tidal that it can run at six or seven knots "upstream", giving boats heading from the sea to the docks a free ride there, and back again. The river flows with the tides all the way up to Teddington Lock, and before the lock was placed on the river, it went further, although with declining strength. No wonder London became such an important port, for the voyage upriver brought goods to the heart of the country's most populous areas, and the Romans, with their extraordinary engineering skill, had identified the area as the furthest downriver stretch where they could feasibly build a bridge. So, bridge, river, sea, and city all came together, a combination formed by geography and population that is unrepeatable anywhere else in the country, and virtually anywhere else in the world. Even those great world cities that are on rivers, such as Paris, Vienna, and Rome, sit on one-way rivers, leaving boats the hard work of beating upstream to get to dock. London's river, and provider, did the work for sailors, as long as they timed their journey correctly. Add this to the food provided by the river, and the danger it posed from flooding, and it's little wonder the early inhabitants of the region sought to propitiate its spirit.

But it's not just the river that links us with this prehistoric period – "London" itself may date from the time before written records. While the city, as city, got going under the Romans, where did the Romans get the name? "London" is not a Latin word, and nor is it English, of course. It derives from the language of the Britons – who would go on to become the Welsh, the Cornish, the Bretons and, in part, the Scots but not the English – and it could mean anything from *laindon* ("long hill"), to *lunnd* ("marsh"), to *lond* ("wild"), with the more fanciful among scholars arguing for it deriving from *kaerlundein* ("Lud's city").

When the Romans did come, in AD 43, they arrived in force. Julius Caesar had made two previous military expeditions to Britain, in 55 and 54 BC, installing a client king in Kent, but he had not annexed the country to the Empire. Claudius, newly arrived on the imperial throne and resting uneasily upon it, needed glory to justify his elevation to the purple. What better way to do that than by conquering a land even the divine Julius had been unable to subdue?

The Thames was the great east–west barrier to an army moving north from its landing points in Kent, but the Romans were nothing if not great military engineers, and the river god withdrew

28

its protection from the natives of Britain. The pattern of the very first Roman roads suggests that the initial Roman crossing over the river was at Westminster, where it was possible to ford the wide and shallow river, and where a makeshift bridge may have been constructed. But once the initial victories were won, the Romans turned to the task of selling subjugation to the native population, and for that they needed cities – Roman civilization was urban and its benefits required concentrations of population to flourish.

So around AD 50, Roman engineers and surveyors, casting around for the best site for a trading settlement on the north bank of the river, found two gravel hills rising fifty feet above the surrounding marshes. Moreover, these stood at a point where the river, although half a mile wide at high tide, was still bridgeable but which ocean-going ships could sail to, using the tidal flow. As a mark of Roman engineering genius, every succeeding bridge has been built within a few feet of this original. The northern end of the bridge was situated where Fish Street Hill now runs up from the river – archaeologists uncovered a Roman pier base here in the 1980s – and the southern side of the bridge found a firm foothold on a sandy island in Southwark, which at the time was mostly mud and water.

The bridge and the river and the city were the trinity that ensured London's prosperity and position through the centuries to come. For the river brought ships from the country and beyond, the bridge provided a way across the great barrier of the Thames and, once built, became the natural focal point for the roads radiating north and south, and the city supplied the people that attracted trade and travellers from the far corners of the world.

The immigrants brought their gods with them, as well as their goods. Gods of the hearth and home, small statues to place upon family altars, protectors in an uncertain world. Every Roman household had a shrine dedicated to the lares and penates, the former invoking the family's ancestors for their protection and blessing, the latter prevailed upon to keep the family fed. In an uncertain world, where death and disaster could erupt at any moment, anything that could be done to turn the odds in your favour was very much worth doing. London itself provides evidence of the precariousness of life and wealth. Just ten years after the city's founding, London was destroyed, its burning by Boudicca and her troops shown tangibly in the foot-thick layer of red remains left by the fire that consumed the wooden houses and shops. The Roman governor, Suetonius, returning from Anglesey where he had been busy pacifying Druids, decided the city was indefensible with the men he had available and left it to burn. The great Roman historian Tacitus describes what happened, and provides the first historical reference to the city.

> This town did not rank as a Roman settlement, but was an important centre for business-men and merchandise. At first, he [Suetonius] hesitated whether to stand and fight there. Eventually, his numerical inferiority – and the price only too clearly paid by the divisional commander's rashness[3] – decided him to sacrifice the single city of Londinium to save the province as a whole. Unmoved by lamentations and appeals, Suetonius gave the signal for departure. The inhabitants were allowed to accompany him. But those who stayed because they were women, or old, or attached to the place, were slaughtered by the enemy.[4]

---

3   The Legio IX Hispana (the Ninth Legion) met Boudicca's men and suffered a catastrophic defeat somewhere near Colchester: the infantry was wiped out and only some of the cavalry escaped. The Ninth proved an ill-starred legion, but the theory, popularized by Rosemary Sutcliff in her book *The Eagle of the Ninth*, that it was finally lost in Caledonia is now disputed, with some historians claiming that the Ninth was sent east and destroyed by Persians rather than Picts.
4   Tacitus, 1956, page 319.

London burned, and not for the last time. But before it burned, its streets ran with blood. The gods of Rome, perhaps all gods, require sacrifice and many lives were sacrificed at the city's foundation, for according to Tacitus "the British did not take or sell prisoners, or practise other war-time exchanges. They could not wait to cut throats, hang, burn, and crucify".[5] The old, the sick, the infirm, those too fearful of leaving, and those too attached, they all died. Many a merchant and trader, staking everything on bringing in a shipment of South Gaulish samian bowls or Central Gaulish glazed vessels for the new market, stayed, fearful of losing a livelihood and, instead, lost a life. So it was the blood of the poor and the outcast and the chancer, chanced, that steeped the foundations from which the second London rose, after Boudicca's defeat and the acceptance of imperial rule. And this is as it should be. London's history, its written history, is a tale of power and riches, but its hidden story and its true foundation are revealed here, in those unable or unwilling to escape the city's first destruction. London eats dreams and dreamers, it consumes the poor, and it began as it would go on.

The city was rebuilt on a grand scale and its significance was confirmed when the emperor Hadrian himself visited in AD 122. The basilica was the largest north of the Alps, at 550 feet (170 metres) square; little remains now but you can see the base of one of the arches by popping into Nicholson and Griffin (barbers) at 90 Gracechurch Street and asking to see the ancient monument – they have to let you in, as it's a public monument. But the very word basilica, in its Roman usage, indicates the basis of imperial religion: a basilica in a Roman town was essentially a combination of town hall and court of law, so the religion of Rome was the state itself. No wonder the city was beautified when the personification of the state, the emperor, came to visit.

---

5   Tacitus, 1956, page 319.

But for ordinary people, the state was terrifying as well as nurturing, its everyday face revealed in the constant round of currying influence and seeking patronage from those higher up the imperial ladder. The gods of hearth and home, the spirits of ancestors, curses and blessings and auguries were all used to try to even out the balance a bit and bring some control, some influence, into the flux of life.

Londoners, a mishmash of peoples from the start, mixed their gods too. Scratched into a first-century flagon are the words: LONDINI AD FANVM ISIDIS ("To London at the temple of Isis"). This temple endured for a further two centuries, being restored in the third century before its altar was finally recycled into a riverside wall. Isis was an Egyptian goddess, an exotic import to go alongside the other exotica to be found in London and, so far, there is no evidence that she was worshipped anywhere in Britain outside the city. But it wasn't just Isis; the goddess brought her consort and her son too, all players in the mystery cults that became popular in London. Other religions organized in secret societies, offering salvation for sacrifice, arrived as well. Cybele, Magna Mater, the Great Mother, was so great that her consort did not need to fertilize her but castrated himself, and her priests did likewise, making eunuchs of themselves with castration clamps – a device that, and I'm not joking, looks suspiciously like a nutcracker. A beautifully decorated castration clamp, complete with small busts of gods, was fished from the Thames in 1840 and is now on display in the British Museum. The fearful device makes Ovid's comment, that the devotees of Cybele filled the air with "loud howls", all the more credible!

There was another Eastern mystery religion too, brought to the capital by immigrants; and I find that my life recapitulates that of the city, for my parents came to London as Christians, from far-flung parts of the world, to study, to settle, and to survive. But there are precious few material or historical traces of Christianity in Roman Londinium. The religion was there, for the bishop of London, one Restitutus, attended a church council in Arles in AD 314. However, as yet no church has been definitely identified, and the only indisputably Christian artefact found in London was a pewter bowl with the Chi-Rho symbol scratched on the bottom. The only other items found so far were lead ingots found in the River Thames near Battersea Bridge, also marked with the Chi-Rho and the inscription "*Spes in deo*" ("hope in God"). Quite what the ingots were doing in the river is anyone's guess, but maybe it's no more complicated than a cack-handed docker dropping them over the side of an unloading boat.

But that's it for Christianity in London. Roman Londoners liked their religion exotic and mysterious, and the strange faith in a man who was crucified and lived again certainly qualified as mysterious, although even stranger was the religion's refusal to accept, even in token form, the required sacrifices to the divine emperor and thus the Roman state. Christianity was brought to Britain by strangers and sojourners, and even after the Roman army left in 410, there is evidence of a Romano-British aristocracy that adhered to the faith in the face of the barbarian invasion: word was sent to the church in Gaul for a bishop to come to preach to those British Christians who had accepted the doctrine of Pelagius (c. 354–c. 420), one of St Augustine's heresiarchs and a native Briton. Bishop Germanus travelled twice to Britain, in 429 and again a few years later, stopping off at the shrine of St Alban and, presumably, London too.

In 410, under attack from Saxons, the Romano-Britons wrote to the emperor Honorius asking for aid in defending the island. The military defences along the Saxon Shore – a string of forts and naval bases along the Channel and east coast designed to intercept raiders from northern Germany and Scandinavia – had been stripped by a pretender to the imperial throne and the island lay all but defenceless against the barbarians. But Honorius had troubles enough of his own: Alans (more fearsome than their name suggests), Vandals, and Suebi had invaded Gaul and Hispania, while in 410 the Visigoths under Alaric sacked Rome itself. Honorius wrote back to the civitates (the civic worthies) of Britain: you're on your own.

And they were. Whereas elsewhere in the Empire the transition from Roman to local rule was marked as much by continuity as change, with the incoming barbarians generally eager to adopt Roman customs and titles, in Britain everything changed. Urban centres decayed and then collapsed completely. Rural villas, which in the third and fourth centuries had become the main dwellings for the wealthy Romano-British aristocracy, were abandoned to the wolves and ravens. Even London, which, judging by its basilica, had once been the greatest imperial city outside Italy, went into steep decline. Cut off from the trade routes that had sustained it, the city cannibalized itself, raising defensive walls from the demolished remains of its own buildings, in a desperate effort to build defences capable of holding off the barbarians.

The Roman Wall around London still exists in many places, but life within the walls slowly ran down during the fifth and sixth centuries, with layers of tilled earth laid on top of demolished buildings, making vegetable plots where once were houses, until, in the end, the city... stopped.

London, for the first and so far only time in its existence, died. Wolves made homes among its ruins, flowers bloomed where the Forum had bustled. Later, the aftercomers looked with wonder upon the works left behind:

> Well-wrought this wall: Weirds broke it.
> The stronghold burst....

Snapped rooftrees, towers fallen,
the work of the Giants, the stonesmiths,
mouldereth.[6]

These are the first lines of "The Ruin", a poem itself in ruins, that exists in a burned and mutilated state in the *Exeter Book*, one of four manuscripts that contain pretty well all the texts to come down to us from the Anglo-Saxon era. The mercenaries called in to protect the Britons from the depredations of the painted people, the Picts, and the Gaels from across the narrow sea, turned upon their employers. Builders in wood, the Angles and the Saxons avoided the stone-built cities and towns of the Romans. But the passing of the old urban life, even though they had themselves largely brought it about, produced both a frisson of supernatural fear and a confirmation of the deepest certainty of the pagan soul: that, in the end, all withers and decays, and death shall have the final word.

"The Ruin" was likely written about the city of Bath, Aquae Sulis of the flowing waters, but it could as much have been Londinium to which it made elegy. However, the city was not dead, but sleeping, and the people who had destroyed it were those who first began to bring it, slowly, back to life.

---

6   Alexander, 1977, page 28.

Chapter 2

NEW GODS FOR OLD

In 1960 an Italian stood in the city of London, in the shadow of St Paul's, and wept. Many centuries earlier, in AD 604, another Italian had stood in the ruins of London and I think he probably wept too. In 1960, the Italian was my mother, newly arrived in London and unable to speak a single word of English, sick with hunger and humiliation as the family she had gone to work for as an au pair all but starved her. Although my mother knew no English, she knew of St Paul's, even from her little village in Piemonte, and on a rare day off she managed to make her way there. Sitting on its steps, looking over the vast city, so different and so indifferent, she wept, thinking of all the decisions and plans that had brought her here, to this strange land. But my mother did not know that the church on whose steps she sat was first founded by an Italian, just as far from home, and just as uncertain of the wisdom of what he was doing.

Back in 604, the Italian who stood on Ludgate Hill, looking around at the tumbledown remains of a once great Roman city, was named Mellitus. And he wept – although I am sure that a man of his gravitas would have kept his tears silent and wept inwardly – he wept from despair at the ruin that lay around him and the magnitude of the task that lay in front of him. He had been made bishop of London, the shepherd of a city that had ceased to exist, and pastor to a people who worshipped, in the view of the Italian, sticks and stones. It was no sort of task for an aristocratic Roman. But it was the task he had been entrusted with and, as Mellitus stood on Ludgate Hill, he must have thought back to the man who had sent him from the cerulean skies of Italy to the fogbound banks of the Thames.

For 200 years London had disappeared into the silence of prehistory. The man who dragged it from the darkness was Italian. His name was Gregory, and he was pope.

In AD 591, as recounted by Bede, Gregory was in Rome and saw, for sale in a slave market, some pale-skinned, fair-haired young men – very different from the olive and black of his own compatriots. When he asked where they hailed from, he was told they were Angles. In a rare example of a pun working as well in translation as in the original, Gregory replied, "Not Angles but angels!" and, on learning that they were pagans, he decided to do something about that, and reclaim for the Church that part of the Empire that had been lost to it.

Gregory dispatched a mission to England, led by Augustine, the prefect of Gregory's own monastery. The missionaries were somewhat less keen on the task appointed them than the man sending them. On their way to Britain, they grew steadily more frightened at the idea of travelling to the ends of the world, to people who not only didn't speak their language but whose manners and customs were notoriously barbarous. So much so, they stopped and Augustine returned to Rome to try to persuade Gregory to rethink this whole mad idea. Gregory did no such thing, but sent Augustine back with a letter to encourage the faint-hearted, and orders to carry on. So, in 597, Augustine and his companions landed in Kent, on what was still the island of Thanet, and were met by the king, Æthelbert, in the open air, for Æthelbert feared that in the dark of a hall these strange men from far away might overwhelm him with their foreign magic. Safe under the sky, the king heard Augustine preach and was sufficiently impressed to grant him land in Canterbury and freedom to preach. Æthelbert's wife, Bertha, was herself foreign, the daughter of King Charibert of the Franks, and as such represented a significant strengthening of ties between Kent and the rising power of the Frankish court.

Power, in the small kingdoms that had proliferated throughout the British Isles in the two centuries following the Empire's collapse, was a delicate, hard-won, and even harder-held prize. Given that its ultimate source was the sword and battle, it might seem strange to call it delicate, but no king reigned on his own, instead relying on a network of alliances with the most powerful families in his kingdom. By marrying abroad, Æthelbert risked alienating some of his supporters – at the very least, he forwent the possibility of tying local support to him through marriage – but he must have calculated that the prestige attached to marrying a descendant of Clovis, the great Merovingian king, more than made up for that. But it was one thing to marry a Frank – it was another thing to accept her religion. For Bertha was Christian, while Æthelbert, like all the Anglo-Saxons and in contrast to the native Britons, was pagan.

The conquest of Britain, although swift in retrospect, was slow at the time, taking centuries. But although slow, it was thorough: the Anglo-Saxons almost completely eradicated the culture that they displaced, replacing an urban, literate, Christian and Roman civilization with a rural, oral, pagan, and Germanic society. While the Britons, driven into the west and on the verge of becoming the Welsh, retained the faith of their fathers and some semblance of Romanitas, the Anglo-Saxons left Roman cities as ruins and put their pigs to root through the shells of country villas, while they sacrificed to their gods on hill and wooded grove. And that is about all we can say for certain about the religion of the Anglo-Saxons.

Everything else is reconstruction. The Anglo-Saxons who first learned to write were the first Christian Anglo-Saxons; whatever records they may have left of the faith of their fathers were almost all destroyed in the great conflagrations that engulfed most of the country's monasteries during the Viking depredations of the ninth and tenth centuries. Archaeology has allowed us to piece together a little – oxen were frequent sacrifices it seems – but most of the rest is derived from extrapolating details of early Germanic and late Norse religion to Anglo-Saxon England. How well that works remains an open question.

Whether impressed by political or spiritual considerations – I suspect the distinction, so beloved of contemporary historians, would have been meaningless to Æthelbert – the king decided to embrace the religion of his wife. This was not a decision without risk, for his eldest son remained pagan, thus creating a potential scission – and rival power centre – in his court. For his part, Augustine was so encouraged by his initial success that he wrote to Pope Gregory, asking him to send more of, well, everything. In response, Gregory sent Mellitus, in 601, as head of a second mission, along with the necessaries for such a mission, including liturgical vessels and vestments, relics, and books. It was to Mellitus that Augustine gave a bishop's hat and – it must have seemed a plum prize when first mooted – the see of the greatest city in the land: London.

Æthelbert's gamble had paid off. He was now the power in the land, the king to whom other kings bowed, and, showing his political muscle, he saw to the conversion to Christianity of his nephew, Sæberht, king of the East Saxons and lord of London. As fruit of that conversion, and to further the mission among the East Saxons, Augustine sent Mellitus to Sæberht with orders to re-establish the bishopric of London.

Standing on Ludgate Hill, Mellitus must have realized that London was most definitely not Rome. But he came as a missionary

40

from a church still rooted in the urban geography of Empire, which planted bishops in cities, and London was the best, indeed the only, candidate for that title in Britain. The next most populous Anglo-Saxon settlement, Southampton, would have comfortably fitted into the baths of Caracalla in Rome.

While the old Roman city had been largely abandoned, a small trading centre had developed a little upriver from Londinium, running along where the Strand now lies and up towards Covent Garden. According to Bede it was a trading centre, and one visited by many people arriving by land and sea. This long puzzled archaeologists, as virtually no trace of early Anglo-Saxon settlement could be found within the City. It was only with further excavations, in the 1980s, that the evidence was uncovered, showing that the Anglo-Saxons, despite the apparent advantages of a still largely intact defensive wall, had founded their settlement about a mile upstream, stretching from where the National Gallery is today to Aldwych.

Why did the Anglo-Saxons avoid living in old Roman-era towns? On the practical level, they were consummate carpenters, but the repair of stone and brick-built buildings was beyond them, so living in Londinium would have entailed the constant risk of a roof or wall falling on their heads. Leaving aside practicality, the abandoned cities and towns of Britain must have seemed wraith-haunted places to them, full of shadows, and telling all too credibly of death and decay. Much better, much less troubling, to build afresh, away from the works of giants.

But Mellitus was a Roman. He was not going to build his church in among hovels when there was a proper city, albeit ruined, just to the east. So, taking a probably reluctant Sæberht with him (kings were no more likely to enter ruined cities than anyone else), Mellitus headed through the gap where a gate in the wall had once been and on, through the ruins, towards the hill that rose above them.

There must have been Christian churches in Londinium, although as yet no trace of them has been found by archaeologists, but it's likely Mellitus too searched for some continuation of the old clergy, some sign that the Mass continued to be offered among the ruins.

My mother, without voice in a strange city, also went searching for religious, and she found them: the Sisters of Verona, who were living in Chiswick in a convent so memorably cold and draughty that even fifty years later it's the first thing my mother recalls. But at least she found a sister who could speak the same language as her, Sister Gesualda, and confirmation that no, it was not accepted practice in England for au pairs to be semi-starved and denied their wages. Continuing the immigrant basis that has usually been apparent in London's religious life, Sister Gesualda, despite her name and fluent Italian, was actually Scottish, having arrived in the capital via long missionary stays in Africa and the Philippines.

Although the Britons maintained the practice of Christianity, there is no record of continuing worship in London. Whatever churches Mellitus might have been able to find were in ruins, their sanctuary lights extinguished, and with the inexpressible sense of presence that is always felt a living church gone.

With no sign of a living church, Mellitus turned to the familiar dead. Rome, too, was a city of ruins, the shadow of its former imperial self, and without the papacy it too might well have been abandoned completely to decay. Even with the popes, and the life-giving pilgrim blood and money they attracted, much of Rome stood empty, stone shadows cast upon cracked pavements, classical temples sending lonely fingers up to the sky. So when Mellitus saw an abandoned temple to the goddess Diana on top of Ludgate Hill, he would suddenly have felt the distance between him and home shrink. It was no wonder that the new bishop of London chose to set up his altar amid the ruins of such a familiar goddess. Diana held no fear for Mellitus. So it was here that Mellitus offered

Mass, amid the ruins, to the new God he and his countrymen were bringing to this strange people.

Mellitus remained in London for ten years. But the mission, that had begun so well, was about to run up against its first great check. For in a time when missions could hardly function without royal patronage and protection – there were no courts, no police, no redress other than the king's sword should brigands be drawn to the accumulated surpluses laid up by the thoughtful, careful husbanding of monks – the death of kings meant all might change. And so it did. In 616, kings Sæberht and Æthelbert died. Sæberht had three sons and they quickly abandoned any pretence they had of following the new, foreign religion and reverted to their old ways, but not without a certain curiosity. For, seeing Mellitus offering Mass, they demanded some of that bread too.

Mellitus, no doubt reflecting on the pressing need for better catechesis, explained that they could only take communion if they had first been baptized. The three brothers were having none of that. They weren't going to get wet, but the reverence surrounding the giving of bread made them think it carried a strong magic – and they wanted that magic. Mellitus, taking this as a teaching moment, continued to explain why communion was impossible without prior baptism, but to no avail.

The brothers, in charge now, weren't about to accept this clerical pettifogging. No bread, no stay.

Having had a bishop for a decade, London was once more bishop- and church-free.

It is a curious feature of Bede's history that, although he was himself convinced that the Roman version of Christianity was correct – orthodox in fact – while the type of Christianity that spread to northern Britain by the efforts of monks from Ireland was in certain aspects – notably when it celebrated Easter – wrong, the Roman missionaries in his history all appear as strangely lacking in fervour when compared to their Celtic brethren. We've already seen that Augustine and his fellows had barely made it out of Italy before they wanted to turn back. Now, having been sent packing from London, Mellitus too decided on the better part of valour. Not for him the red crown of the martyr; he was heading back, if not home, then at least across the Channel to Gaul, where they had decent wine.

He was joined in Gaul by Justus, the bishop of Rochester in Kent, for Æthelbert's son, Eadbald, had likewise apostatized, taking as his wife Æthelbert's widow (not Bertha – she had died some time before Æthelbert, and the king had remarried). This frankly rather icky marriage was forbidden under church law – one dreads to think of the pillow talk between Eadbald and his wife – but Eadbald had probably entered into the marriage to shore up a rather shaky reign, tying a powerful clan to him by marriage as his father had done.

Maybe centuries of being sent off by their mothers with the injunction to return with their shields or on them had exhausted Italian military fervour. It was certainly true that when the Second World War started, very few displayed any enthusiasm at all for the Duce's ambitions. My own grandfather, when called up, leafed through the booklet on health exemptions and, finding that a certain number of teeth were deemed necessary for the fighting man, repaired to a room on his own with a pair of pliers and a bottle of grappa, thus escaping enlistment at the price of the mother of all hangovers – and a gap-toothed smile.

Augustine himself had died in 604 and Laurence succeeded him as archbishop of Canterbury. Pope Gregory's original intention had been for there to be two archbishoprics in the country, in London and York, corresponding to the main civilian and military centres of Roman Britain. But, not surprisingly, Æthelbert was unwilling to let the archbishop pass from his immediate area of control, nor would he have been able to protect him elsewhere. So Laurence remained in Canterbury and, ever since, the bishop of a small town in Kent has ranked first among the prelates of England.

However, with Æthelbert's death and Eadbald's readoption of pagan practices to go with his forbidden wife, Archbishop Laurence decided to follow his brother bishops, Mellitus and Justus, into exile. It was surely better to go somewhere where he could serve God, rather than remain among pagans who rejected his message.

So what had begun so well was on the point of complete collapse. Laurence retired to bed, ready to take ship to Gaul the next day, when an irate St Peter appeared to him and set about whipping the cowardly cleric. Peter pointed out, in between strokes of the lash, that he had been imprisoned, beaten, whipped and, finally, crucified for the sake of the Faith and the people set under his care, while Laurence and his fellow bishops were set on fleeing because the Anglo-Saxons were not listening to them with sufficient respect.

The next morning, an abashed Laurence went to see King Eadbald and, showing him the weals on his back and sides, pointed out the power of the apostle who had thus lashed him and, by implication, that of the God Peter served. According to Bede, Eadbald, alarmed by this demonstration of divine power, received baptism, put aside his unlawful wife, and set about promoting Christianity in Kent, sending messengers across the Channel to recall bishops Mellitus and Justus. Back in England, Justus resumed the bishopric of Rochester but the Londoners were not prepared to take Mellitus back; the city had reverted to paganism. It was not until 675 that it would definitely have a bishop again: Earconwald.

As for Mellitus, he became archbishop of Canterbury after Laurence died, and was a noted sufferer from gout. Bede tells how Mellitus was carried on his sickbed in Canterbury, where he lay crippled with his gout, when the call of "Fire!" went up. Seeing the flames about to engulf church and town, he prayed with such fervour that the wind swung north, blowing the fire back whence it had come, and then dropped away to nothing. So, with his episcopal see still intact, Mellitus went the way of all flesh on 24 April 624, the first of the patron saints of London.

There is something gloriously appropriate that the first of the city's patron saints should be an immigrant and then an exile, a sufferer from gout (and while I know there are other causes of the condition apart from excess wine and rich foods, I like to think that St Mellitus enjoyed them well), and a fireman. These four – immigrants, exiles, consumption, and fire – have always been drivers of the city and, in St Mellitus, we have a true patron of London.

The mission had survived, thanks to St Peter and his whip, but after its initial glorious promise, it seemed to be dying slowly away. To any outside observer wanting to put his bet with the smart money, the old gods would have seemed the better wager; the people of London, despite its decline still the largest concentration of people in the country, had tried both and opted for Woden and Thunor, the gods of battle. And no wonder. This was an age where the truth of theology was tested in battle; a god that could not give victory on the battlefield was not worth a prayer. As such, why should the Anglo-Saxons adopt the god of the people they had already defeated in claiming their new kingdoms? Christ was the God of the beaten Britons, driven into exile in Brittany or into the mountains of Wales and the north.

The short answer: Jesus jumped sides, and started fighting for the Anglo-Saxons.

The slightly longer answer: through a combination of battles and marriage alliances, power in seventh-century Britain shifted to the northern kingdom of Northumbria, whose kings had, while in exile in Ireland, become Christians. Returning, and claiming the throne of Northumbria, the successive kings Oswald and Oswiu (who were brothers) invited monks from Iona to set up a monastery on Lindisfarne. This rapidly became a great centre of learning and the training school for generations of missionary monks. And as the most powerful kings in the land, Oswald and Oswiu had the political and military muscle to protect the new church.

However, it's worth mentioning that the Anglo-Saxons converted freely and of their own choice. When faced with a choice between their old pagan gods and this new God from across the sea, they chose, over the space of a couple of generations, to follow these new ways, even though by doing so they were accepting the religion of the defeated Britons.

While the battle for England's soul was fought out, London largely went its own way. Cedd is often listed as the next bishop of London, but this Northumbrian was rather the bishop of the East Saxons. A monk of the Iona/Lindisfarne school, he saw his duties as tending to a people – the East Saxons – rather than being bishop of a place. Wine comes after Cedd in the list of bishops of London, but likewise he had little to do with the city. It was only with Earconwald, who accepted the pallium around 675, that the line of resident London bishops resumes. But more interesting than Earconwald is the extraordinary man who made him into a bishop, Theodore.

The phrase that accompanies his name gives away something of what made Theodore so remarkable: of Tarsus. Theodore of Tarsus. Tarsus, in modern-day Turkey but then part of the Greek-speaking world, is a long way from England. So how did a Greek end up as archbishop of Canterbury?

Tarsus lay near Antioch, a city renowned for the intellectual rigour of its scholars. Theodore was born in 602 and studied at Antioch, learning the distinctive style of biblical exegesis practised in the city, an analytical style that strove to uncover the precise literal meaning of biblical texts through the careful application of grammar, rhetoric, and philosophy. Through his immersion in the school of Antioch, Theodore gained an impressive mastery over a huge range of scholarly disciplines. But the seventh century was a time of turmoil in the East, with the empires of Byzantium and Persia exhausting each other in a series of wars, only for the Persian Sassanid Empire to be brought crashing down by the eruption of the tribes of the Arabian peninsula, who had united under the flag of holy war in the name of a new religion: Islam. For their part, the Byzantines buckled but they did not break, and the Arab advance spread west and east, stymied for centuries by the walls of Constantinople. However, in the face of such invasions, the safest place to be was definitely behind the walls, and Theodore made his way to the imperial city and then, for reasons unknown, on to Rome.

By the time Theodore emerged from monkish obscurity into historical documents, he had already lived a full and, for the time, long life. He was in his sixties and no doubt, after the various trials and upheavals that had brought him to Rome, expected to live out the rest of his life there. But that was not to be his fate.

Wigheard, the new archbishop of Canterbury, had arrived in Rome to receive his pallium (the insignia of his office as metropolitan) but died of the plague there in 667, leaving Pope Vitalian (r.657–672) with a body and a vacancy on his hands. Burying the body, he set about filling the vacancy, offering it to Hadrian, one of his counsellors and abbot of a monastery near Naples. Hadrian declined the post, but put Theodore's name forward. The pope accepted his suggestion, with the proviso that Hadrian accompany Theodore to England. Hoisted by his own recommendation, Hadrian had to agree.

Their departure was delayed while Theodore grew out his hair – Greek monks were tonsured by completely shaving their heads, while Western monks shaved crown and sides, leaving a ring of hair around their heads. Once Theodore had grown enough hair to shave most of it off again, Pope Vitalian consecrated him bishop on 26 March 668. With Hadrian, he set off on the long journey north on 27 May 668, arriving exactly a year later. Theodore was sixty-seven years old.

He was also a man in a hurry. With Hadrian, he set out on an immediate tour of his archdiocese, which had fallen into some disarray, with only three bishops in office. Theodore set about filling vacancies, reorganizing and breaking up overly large dioceses, and summoning regular synods, while setting up a school in Canterbury to teach the scholarly disciplines with which he and Hadrian were familiar. So successful were they in their teaching that Bede tells us of some of their students, still alive in his day, who were as fluent in Greek and Latin as they were in English.

It was Theodore, the Greek from Rome, who decisively remodelled the church in England, fixing its diocesan structure and ensuring that bishops, where possible urban bishops, wielded authority rather than abbots of monasteries.

Theodore eventually died, aged eighty-eight, a very, very long way from where he had been born and lived most of his life. The final twenty-one years of his life, spent in a north-western corner of the world that he can never have expected to visit, were extraordinarily productive in terms of scholarship, leadership, and formation, leading many later Anglo-Saxons to view it as something of a golden age.

Theodore died in 690, nearly a century after Augustine had landed in Kent, and with his death passed a remarkable century in which the popes in Rome had played a decisive, although long-distance, role in the Christianization of the Anglo-Saxons. As we have seen, when faced with a choice between Christianity and the old gods of their forefathers, the Anglo-Saxons freely chose the new God from the East. Some contemporary attempts to reconstruct the old Anglo-Saxon religion seem to be as much about explaining away such a decision as trying to understand why they made the choice they did.

For my part, and though such a crucial decision will have had many components, there seems little reason to doubt that a large part of it was as Bede claimed. For when writing of a crucial meeting called to decide whether or not to accept Christianity, he puts into the mouth of an unnamed thegn this account of the bleakness and nobility of the old pagan world view, and the hope that had flown among them:

> When we compare the present life of man on earth with that time of which we have no knowledge, it seems to me like the swift flight of a single sparrow through the banqueting-hall where you are sitting at dinner on a winter's day with your thegns and counsellors. In the midst there is a comforting fire to warm the hall; outside, the storms of winter rain or snow are raging. This sparrow flies swiftly in through one door of the hall, and out through another. While he is inside, he is safe from the winter storms; but after a few moments of comfort, he vanishes from sight into the wintry world from which he came. Even so, man appears on earth for a little while; but of what went before this life or of what follows, we know nothing. Therefore, if this new teaching has brought any more certain knowledge, it seems only right that we should follow it.[7]

Nobility and pathos were found in the old pagan world view, but there was precious little hope. Nor was there much choice for the sons and daughters of the nobility beyond weapons training and war, and marriage. Christianity gave hope, and a whole new set of possibilities; a son might take up a pen rather than a sword, a daughter might enter a joint monastery and become, in time, its head, ruling over men and women.

But how deeply had Christianity penetrated into wider, and poorer, Anglo-Saxon society by the time of Theodore's death? In

---

7   Bede, 1990, pages 129–30.

this matter, the dead speak louder than the living. Think of the magnificent Sutton Hoo burial. It is magnificent because of what the living have sent to the grave to accompany the dead man, most probably King Rædwald of the East Angles. He died around 624. But even poor men were not sent to the afterlife without goods. This was the characteristic feature of pagan burials, whereas with Christian burials it was impossible to tell whether the dead man was a king or a slave.

So, what happens with the dead? By the late seventh century, the practice of packing stuff in with the dead has declined, with 45 per cent of burials bare and 25 per cent furnished only with knives. "Around the 720s, the deposition of all non-perishable grave-goods, except occasional knives, finally ended."[8]

As far as the dead were concerned, the Anglo-Saxons were Christian.

But while the Anglo-Saxons had accepted the religion of the people they had conquered, their cousins across the sea had not, and in AD 793, amid portents and signs, comets and dragons flaming in the sky, the Viking Age began. And it began as it was to continue, in fire and blood, in slaves taken and plunder looted. The Northmen attacked Lindisfarne, the holiest site in Anglo-Saxon England, and the shock of desecration echoed around Europe. Anglo-Saxon scholars and missionaries, taking up the baton passed to them by the Irish, had set out to bring the news of hope to their own people across the grey sea, sending missionaries to the tribal peoples of north-western Europe, while Charlemagne harvested the fruit of Anglo-Saxon scholarship for his Carolingian Renaissance among the Franks. So when news of the attack on Lindisfarne reached Charlemagne's court, the Northumbrian scholar Alcuin responded, by letter, with outrage and amazement.

---

8   Blair, 2005, page 240.

Lo, it is nearly 350 years that we and our fathers have inhabited this most lovely land, and never before has such terror appeared in Britain as we have now suffered from a pagan race, nor was it thought that such an inroad from the sea could be made. Behold, the church of St Cuthbert spattered with the blood of the priests of God, despoiled of all its ornaments; a place more venerable than all in Britain is given as a prey to pagan peoples.[9]

But this was only the start. With their incomparable longships and desire for plunder, the coastal, poorly defended monasteries must have seemed to the Vikings like an all-you-can-eat smörgåsbord. Indeed, the carefully spaced regularity of some of the attacks suggests that the Vikings were, in effect, farming the monasteries, waiting long enough after one attack for a fresh crop of monks and religious artefacts to be sown before attacking again. For while gold was great, monks, sold as slaves in the slave markets of the Viking trading centre at Dublin, were no less valuable a resource.

As the attacks continued, the Anglo-Saxon kingdoms slowly frayed and crumbled until, in AD 865, what *The Anglo-Saxon Chronicle* called "a great heathen army" landed in East Anglia. And there, it waited.

The peace, if such it was, lasted a year, while Edmund, king of the East Angles, bought off the invaders with gold and horses. But the leaders of this Great Army had not come for swift profit and sudden escape: they had come to conquer. As 866 wound down towards autumn, the dragon stirred and, with sudden ferocity, turned north, destroying in a few months' campaigning the ancient kingdom of Northumbria and, according to some scholars, sacrificing its king to the Norse gods via the rite of the blood eagle. This meant the ribs of the unfortunate king were prised apart and

---

9   Whitelock, 1979, page 842.

the lungs pulled from the still living man, to be draped over his shoulders in a grotesque mockery of wings.

Too fearful to intervene, the remaining Anglo-Saxon kingdoms – East Anglia, Mercia, and Wessex – looked on, wondering where next the dragon would turn its gaze. When the Army stirred again, it fell upon the kingdom of the East Angles.

> This year [869] the army rode over Mercia into East-Anglia, and there fixed their winter-quarters at Thetford. And in the winter King Edmund fought with them; but the Danes gained the victory, and slew the king; whereupon they overran all that land.[10]

Mercia was next, and it duly fell, its king abdicating his throne and going into exile rather than facing the unstoppable might of the Great Heathen Army.

In five years, the Viking army had conquered what it had taken the Anglo-Saxons centuries to overcome. Now only Wessex remained and it was surely only a matter of time before it was conquered too. The old king was dead, and of his sons just two remained alive: Æthelred, and a young man, just twenty-one, who had never been expected to take the throne: Alfred.

London played a crucial but obscure part in Alfred's great struggle with the Vikings. It seems, from hints in the historical record, that the bridge first built by the Romans had been repaired over the centuries so that it still stood. No doubt spring surges and, just as dangerous to a wooden structure, fires caused sections to collapse, but it seems to have been regularly rebuilt. The Vikings were traders as much as they were raiders, so London, with its ease of access by boat and continuing trading network, was of great interest to them. So they took it. It was the winter of 871–72 and the city remained

---

10   Quote from *The Anglo-Saxon Chronicle* (translated by James Ingram).

under their control until 886, when Alfred retook it. During that time, Alfred had won some battles and lost more. He'd been driven, a fugitive, into hiding in the marshes of the Somerset Levels, and there into myth, only to re-emerge into history to inflict a decisive defeat on the Viking army at the Battle of Edington in 878. From there, he advanced eastwards until "Alfred occupied London, and all the English people submitted to him, except those who were in captivity to the Danes; and he then entrusted the city to ealdorman Æthelred to rule."[11]

If Alfred had simply been a general, he would have been notable enough, but victory – for a time – over the Vikings was the spur to a quite remarkable outpouring of political and scholarly genius (and I do not use the word lightly). If there was one thing Alfred's long struggle against the Vikings had taught him, it was that victory, and peace, was temporary. The Northmen would be back. But Alfred was determined to be ready for them next time.

So he set about the most fundamental reorganization of England since the Romans. Reasoning that the great strategic advantage held by the Vikings was their ability to launch surprise attacks and then withdraw on their longboats, Alfred created through the length and breadth of his kingdom a network of towns, burhs, fortified by wooden palisades and ditches, and so placed that all his subjects could reach safety within a day. Some of these burhs used existing Roman defences, others were built from scratch, but what Alfred effectively did was plant the first towns in England since the withdrawal of the legions.

The Anglo-Saxon settlement of London already existed but, having grown up along the strand, it was acutely vulnerable. So, Alfred moved London back within the old city walls, where it could better resist Viking attack.

---

11   From *The Anglo-Saxon Chronicle*, quoted in Inwood, 1998, page 38.

To go with the fixed defences he had built throughout the kingdom, Alfred reorganized the army, establishing a mobile force that was permanently ready to deal with any Viking incursions, rather than having to call men from their fields, which had ensured that by the time enough were assembled the raiders had long gone.

But Alfred was, first and foremost, a Christian king. In analysing the reason for the Viking attacks, and their success, he looked to understand why God had permitted such a scourge to fall upon his people and the people of England. Extraordinarily, he concluded it was because the English had allowed their love of learning and scholarship to wither and decay. Looking around, Alfred saw a country, which had once been renowned as the foremost intellectual centre of northern Europe, now unable to produce even a handful of competent Latinists. This seems to be true, for even at Canterbury, the surviving Latin texts of the time reveal that whoever was writing them was almost completely ignorant of the language. The contrast with the time of Theodore and Hadrian, when the church in England boasted men as fluent in Greek and Latin as English, could not have been starker.

So, with characteristic boldness, Alfred set about renewing learning. He imported scholars from elsewhere in Britain and abroad, and he set them to the task of translating into English "certain books which are the most necessary for all men to know".[12] And to show how serious he was about all this, Alfred learned Latin himself and set about doing some of the translating. Thus, and uniquely for a king of this era, we have Alfred's own thoughts – because he could not resist interpolating them in the texts he was translating – on topics ranging from the qualities required of a king through to the difficulty of finding loyal friends.

---

12   Keynes and Lapidge, 2004, page 126.

All this preparation bore fruit, for when the Vikings did return, in the 890s, the Anglo-Saxons were ready for them. An increasingly demoralized army of would-be raiders was hounded from one side of the country to the other until finally it gave up in disgust and went off to seek easier treasure elsewhere.

Alfred died in 899 but his remarkable son and daughter, Edward the Elder and Æthelflæd, Lady of the Mercians, continued the strategy he had developed. Gradually they reclaimed the Danelaw, that part of Britain settled by the Northmen and ruled by them, until finally Alfred's grandson, Athelstan, became the first true king of England.

If it sounds as if I've got a bit of a crush on Alfred, I plead guilty. The Victorians venerated him as the perfect king, but later generations have consigned him to a barely remembered folk tale of burnt cakes. Maybe he is too pious for modern tastes, but I find his deep search for the right path in the extraordinarily violent world in which he lived hugely relevant to modern times. Besides, Alfred loved books, with the deep passion of a time when books were rare and all the more precious for that.

Alfred and his children and grandson earned England – for England now recognizably existed – a century of peace.

Through that time, London was still served by only a handful of churches: St Paul's, All-Hallows-by-the-Tower, St Andrew Holborn, and St Bride's Fleet Street, with St Alban Wood Street, St Mary-le-Bow, and St Peter Cornhill as other possibilities. Not very many for a city that had grown greatly during the century. Priests were still too few for a parish system – little local churches serving local communities – to be feasible. Instead, large monastic churches – minsters – with teams of monks and priests were responsible for large areas, and from the minsters priests and monks went out to bury, baptize, and preach. Anglo-Saxon priests functioned more like sixteenth-century Jesuits, on their far-flung missionary journeys, than thirteenth-century rectors, with their intimate knowledge of the doings of a small parish. Even in London, there were not enough clergy for a fully fledged parochial system. But as the ninth century, with its Viking wars, passed into the relative peace of the tenth century, priestly numbers slowly increased in common with a general rise in population.

All were to be tested again, though, as the tenth century turned into the eleventh and England found itself ruled by the most incompetent monarch ever to take the throne: Æthelred. There have been worse men as kings – in terms of personal brutality it's hard to beat a man who executes his own wives, but at least Henry VIII maintained the kingdom. If the first and most fundamental duty of a king is the defence of the realm, then Æthelred failed, and failed abjectly. The Vikings were back, and instead of meeting them in battle, Æthelred paid them off, again and again and again, with the raiders demanding more each time. The kingdom was bled dry.

In the end, Æthelred was driven into exile by the Danish king, Swein Forkbeard. Calling on his ally, Olaf, the king of Norway, Æthelred returned, although he needed Olaf to do the fighting for him. Finding Swein's army holding London Bridge, Olaf had his men tie hawsers to the bridge supports and row, row, row, muscles bulging and throats bursting, until they pulled the bridge, with Swein's army, down.

Olaf was a new breed of Viking: a Christian Viking. Christianity does not seem to have significantly reduced the violence of Viking kings but at least more of their exploits were written down. In gratitude to their saviour, Londoners consecrated a slew of churches to Olaf in the early decades of the eleventh century, including St Olave's Church Southwark and, probably, St Olave Hart Street. Indeed, the Danes, having embraced Christianity, espoused it with fervour, initiating the explosion of church-building that would go on to transform London in the eleventh and twelfth centuries. At the start of the eleventh century there were maybe seven churches serving the city but by 1170 there were 126 parish churches and thirteen conventual churches serving city and suburbs. These churches reflected the wealth of the patrons who paid for their building – and given the amount of money extorted by the Viking incursions against Æthelred's England, it's not surprising that many of them were Danish institutions. But others marked a late outpouring – possibly desperate – of Anglo-Saxon piety, and then there were some Norman institutions, of which the most notable surviving example is St Bartholomew-the-Great.

Æthelred finally died, unlamented, in 1016 and Cnut, the son of Swein Forkbeard, took control of the country after a brief struggle with Æthelred's son, Edmund Ironside. Danish control only lasted twenty-six years. In 1042, Æthelred's son Edward "the Confessor" returned from exile in Normandy to become king. His great significance for London's religious life was his decision to rebuild a monastic church upon marshy Thorney Island, upstream from the city, an island formed by the forking of the Tyburn as it flowed into the Thames. The new minster, lying to the west of the city, became Westminster Abbey, and Edward moved his royal residence from the city to the environs of his new abbey church, thus creating the west–east tension between London's political and commercial centres that has characterized the city's life and growth ever since.

Edward built his church in the new Romanesque style, spending on it "a tenth of his entire substance in gold, silver, cattle and all other possessions",[13] although that did not save it from Henry II, who almost completely demolished the Confessor's church when rebuilding it in the snazzy new Gothic style.

English history has a very convenient and universally remembered date for the transition from the Early Medieval (what

---

13   Hunting, 1981, page 21.

used to be called the Dark Ages), to the full-blown Medieval: 1066. Before the Conquest, kings were labelled by appellations: Æthelred "the Unready", Edward "the Confessor", Edgar "the Peaceable". After, they were numbered. Before, they had names like Eadwig and Æthelstan. After, they were called William and Henry.

England was about to be thoroughly Frenchified.

CHAPTER 3

A TIME FOR GIFTS

As far as I can see, it was always winter in the medieval period. At least, that's how it seems in pretty well every film I've seen set then. Always winter, usually raining, perpetually grey, and certainly never, ever Christmas. It's as if the White Witch ensorcelled an entire era.

It wasn't like that. The medievals loved colour: they painted everything they could get their hands on, dyed their clothes, and coloured their windows, so even light became saturated with colour. As for the eternal winter, in fact they lived through the Medieval Warm Period, so while there were certainly still winters, the summers were hotter, longer, and more predictable than in the succeeding centuries. In fact, early Hollywood, with its men in tights, Technicolor saturation, and assignations in gloriously verdant forest glades, was probably more accurate in its depiction of medieval times than contemporary film-makers: think *The Adventures of Robin Hood* over *The Name of the Rose*.

But even colouring everything in imagination, medieval London remains distant. Although it would not have seemed so to the people living between 1066 and 1485 (the conventional dates for the Middle Ages in England, beginning with the Conquest and finishing with the end of the Wars of the Roses and the accession of the House of Tudor), seeing as how they had to deal with the Black Death, Crusades, and wars internal and external, still this was the most stable period of London's long history. Apart from a fairly brief interlude when Jews lived in the city – of which more below – London was a city with a single faith and one church; very different from before and after. So while the arches and buttresses, the severely upright figures and kaleidoscopic colours of medieval architecture are, to my mind, humanity's greatest achievement in stone and place, yet this period stands apart from me, a vivid counterpoint to London's usual cacophony of competing beliefs. While more remains, physically, of medieval London than its Roman and Anglo-Saxon versions, yet it seems more distant to us: a remote mirror, angled away. So I won't stop too long in the London of Chaucer and Dick Whittington, but we can still take a while to wander its streets and visit its churches, to learn something of the religious life of what was now, indisputably, England's greatest city.

But before that, for two centuries, from shortly after the Conquest to 1290, there was a thread running through the cloth of Christian London, a Jewish thread. There is no record of any Jewish population in Anglo-Saxon England, but William invited Jews, from Rouen in Normandy, to England soon after the Conquest. Usury, the lending of money at interest, was forbidden under Church law but permitted for Jews. In fact, since they were unable to own land, and entrance to the medieval craft guilds was barred to them, moneylending and medicine, along with pawn broking, were about all the activities allowed to London's Jewish population.

The newcomers settled on the north side of Cheapside, their presence still commemorated in the road, Old Jewry, and the church St Lawrence Jewry. And, at first, the relationship between the communities seems to have been curious and even cordial. In 1092, Gilbert Crispin, the abbot of Westminster, wrote to Archbishop Anselm in Canterbury (the man responsible for the ontological proof of God's existence, the most logically watertight and least viscerally convincing of all the rational arguments for God) of his discussions with a London Jew:

> I wrote it recently, putting to paper what a Jew said when formerly disputing with me against our faith in defence of his own law, and what I replied in favour of the faith against his objections. I know not where he was born, but he was educated at Mayence; he was well versed even in our law and literature, and had a mind practised in the Scriptures and in disputes against us. He often used to come to me as a friend both for business and to see me, since in certain things I was very necessary to him, and as often as we came together we would soon get talking in a friendly spirit about the Scriptures and our faith. Now on a certain day, God granted both him and me greater leisure than usual, and soon we began questioning as usual. And as his objections were consequent and logical, and as he explained with equal consequence his former objections, while our reply met his objections foot to foot, and by his own confession seemed equally supported by the testimony of the Scriptures, some of the bystanders requested me to preserve our disputes as likely to be of use to others in future.[14]

Crispin goes on to give the arguments of his Jewish interlocutor in an account that is notable for its fair-mindedness and calm – no trace here of the hysteria that tinges so many later sources. Indeed, under William and his immediate successors, in particular Henry I, London's Jewish population was positively privileged, with the oath of a Jew worth that of twelve Christians. In fact, under Henry I, Aaron of Lincoln became the king's chief moneylender, working

---

14 Jacobs, 1893, pages 7–8.

with a network of Jewish agents throughout the country to bankroll the king's expenditure as well as financing the building of many monasteries, particularly those of the Cistercians. Aaron became so wealthy that he reputedly grew richer than the king. However, indicating the precarious nature of Jewish existence, on Aaron's death all his money was seized by the Crown, on the grounds that as a usurer, his estate was escheat to the king. All money gained through usury reverted to the Crown on the death of the usurer, whether Christian or Jew, but since Christians were debarred from lending money at interest, this law when applied to the Jews provided major windfalls to perpetually cash-strapped kings.

However, their position slowly deteriorated, with the blood libel – the rumour that Jews kidnapped, killed, and used the blood of Christian children in their rituals – first being circulated in the latter part of the twelfth century. Then, when Richard I acceded to the throne, a party of prominent Jews came to pay homage to him at his coronation at Westminster Abbey on 3 September 1189. When the king refused to meet them – he didn't allow women into the ceremony either, so Richard's prejudices seem to have been fairly broad – a rumour spread that Richard had authorized their massacre and a mob gathered in Old Jewry, attacking the homes there. The houses were too strong to be stormed, but they could not resist fire, and the people sheltering in them were burned to death. Richard was enraged at this assault, although probably more because, by this time, the status of Jews in England had been settled as that of king's men, like the Norman barons, and an assault on the Jews of London was an indirect assault on him. However, Richard, set on crusade, made little effort to catch the perpetrators of the London massacre. As king's men, Jews had the right to move and settle anywhere they chose, under the king's protection, but in return for this protection the Angevin kings grew to look more and more on England's Jews as their personal bank, to be raided whenever they needed money – and they always needed money. When Richard was taken hostage by Henry VI, the Holy Roman Emperor, on his way home from the Crusades, the Jews of England had to pay 5,000 marks towards his ransom, three times the amount the City of London contributed.

Although the kings who reigned after Richard squeezed the Jews harder for money, they found them less and less forthcoming: their demands were bleeding the community dry. But since Jews could provide less towards the Royal Exchequer, they became less valuable to the Crown, particularly when new, Christian, moneylenders (step forward, my Italian ancestors!) began moving into town. Then, in 1275, Edward I issued the Statute of the Jewry, forbidding Jews to earn living from moneylending, as well as restricting their abode to certain towns and requiring them to wear a yellow identity badge sewn upon their clothing. The statute further required the country's Jews, within fifteen years of the law's proclamation, to be making their living as farmers, merchants, craftsmen, or soldiers. But farming is not a skill easily acquired, the medieval craft guilds would not accept Jews, and few wanted to become tailors or carpenters, let alone soldiers. So, in 1290, Edward issued the Edict of Expulsion: the community that had enjoyed early wealth and honour and then endured increasing persecution through two centuries was expelled.

They left behind only their dead, in the Jewish cemetery at Cripplegate that, until 1177, was the only licensed resting place for Jews in the kingdom; so it received the dead from communities around the country. Archaeologists, when they investigated the site in 1961, found only empty graves and the skeleton of a dog, perhaps indicating that the site had been desecrated after the Jews left the country. No tombstones were found during the dig, but parts of six were found when sections of the city wall were demolished through the centuries: they had been recycled into the city's defences. They were later lost, and the inscriptions were not transcribed particularly well, but the stone found in Ludgate probably read: "Here lies Rabbi Moses, son of the honourable Rabbi Isaac".

With the departure of the rabbi's co-religionists, the 200-year sojourn of Jews in medieval England ended and London returned to the single faith and single church that characterized it through the Middle Ages.

But while there was one Church, the city had many churches. The frenzy of church-building in late Anglo-Saxon and early Norman times meant that the city was thoroughly supplied with places to worship. What was left to do was the beautification of these churches, the turning of places of stone into pedagogical instruments through painting, sculpture, and glass. At a time when literacy was still far from common (although it was more widespread in London than elsewhere, as the city's merchant classes needed to be able to read and write), the interiors of churches were the most obvious places to teach men and women the basic elements of Christian belief. It's almost impossible to imagine how vivid these churches must have been: five centuries of iconoclasm have whitewashed our memories and scrubbed the surviving medieval churches of their colour. To get some idea of what even simple parish churches must have looked like, think of the Basilica of St Francis in Assisi, with its sky-blue ceiling and astonishing frescoes by Giotto, Cimabue, and Simone Martini. While London's parish churches likely did not have access to artists as talented as Giotto, yet the overwhelming colour, the sheer life breathed into stone, gives some idea of what medieval London churches would have been like.

The religion they practised was just as vivid; the weft that threaded the warp of every aspect of London's life, from the guilds that attempted to regulate the crafts and trades through to baking. (Archaeologists have found a ceramic sweetmeat mould that, when baked, would have transformed the encased doughy mixture into an edible St Catherine of Alexandria – she of Catherine wheel fame.) Medieval Christianity was as intensely physical as it was spiritual, and the two aspects come together perfectly in a fifteenth-century finger ring, which was plain on the outside but engraved on the inside – the skin side – with images of the Trinity, the Virgin and Child, and St Thomas Becket: the holy in constant contact with the physical.

Although the Church was an overarching and possibly overwhelming presence in medieval London, yet there were safety valves, from the boy elected as bishop on the feast of St Nicholas on 6 December, whose authority ran, symbolically at least, until the feast of the Holy Innocents on 28 December, to the Lord of Misrule, who reigned from Hallowe'en to Candlemas (2 February). The great London historian, John Stow, described the Lord of Misrule in his *Survey of London*:

> ... first in the feast of Christmas, there was in the king's house, wheresoever he was lodged, a Lord of Misrule, or Master of merry disports, and the like was to be found in the house of every noble man, of honour or good worship, be he a lord spiritual or temporal. Among these was the Mayor of London, as well as the sheriffs, and each had their Lords of Misrule, ever contending without quarrel or offence who should make the rarest pastimes to delight the beholders. These Lords began their rule on All Hallows' Eve and continued the same until the day after the Feast of Purification, commonly called Candlemas Day [2 February]. In all this time there were fine and subtle disguisings, masks and mummeries, with playing at cards for counters, nails and points in every house, more for pastimes than for gain.[15]

15 Stow, 1908, page 37.

The Church's overwhelming presence in medieval life was made physical in St Paul's Cathedral. This vast building dominated London in a way that even its successor, Wren's cathedral, built after the Great Fire, did not, for Old St Paul's was longer, wider and, most importantly, taller than its replacement. The church was first begun in the eleventh century under William I, after the previous cathedral had also burned down, but it took a couple of centuries to complete. When it was done – in a style that began in heavy Norman Romanesque and ended in English Gothic – it sat upon Ludgate Hill, piercing the sky with a wooden spire that, traditionally, rose 489 feet into the air. In fact, the whole roof was made of wood, lightening the structure but eventually dooming it. So big was Old St Paul's that the route north/south through the transepts became an accepted public thoroughfare to avoid making the long detour around the whole of the church, and so long was its nave that walking it became a pastime, reaching its zenith after the Reformation when Paul's Walk became the accepted place for catching up with City gossip and fashion. While the medieval clergy may have been spared the sight of gallants cavorting down the aisle (Thomas Dekker devotes a whole chapter of *The Gull's Hornbook* to "How a Gallant should behave himself in Paul's Walks") they had crosses of their own to bear. In the fourteenth century, Bishop Braybrook (bishop of London from 1381 to 1404) complained:

> In our Cathedral, not only men, women also, not on common days alone but especially on Festivals, expose their wares, as it were, in a public market, buy and sell without reverence for the holy place... Others, too, by the instigation of the devil, do not scruple with stones and arrows to bring down the birds, pigeons, and jackdaws which nestle in the walls and crevices of the building: others play at ball or at other unseemly games,

both within and without the church, breaking the beautiful and costly painted windows to the amazement of the spectators.[16]

However big St Paul's was, it could not hold the whole population of London, and sometimes the whole population – or a fair section of it – needed to hear what was said at the cathedral. So on its grounds a cross was erected, with a platform upon which a priest or bishop could stand and address the multitudes. From Paul's Cross, Henry III reassured Londoners that he would respect their ancient privileges, excommunications were pronounced, proclamations were made and, sometimes, witches were tried, most notably Richard Walker, a chaplain in Worcester. Having been found in possession of two books of images, Walker was found guilty of witchcraft in 1422. Now of course, this being medieval London, surely he would have been summarily executed and burned at the stake, since wasn't that what they did to witches then? Well, no. The great witch craze was no medieval frenzy, but a product of the Renaissance and after: it reached a peak between 1580 and 1630. The fortunate Rev. Walker, being a medieval cleric, was simply paraded along Cheapside with the books hanging from his head and back, and then, when he returned to the cathedral, the offending books were burned and he was released. Paul's Cross would go on to play a part in the religious turmoil of the Tudor years before being finally demolished in 1643. In 1910, a new cross was set up on the site of the old one. Standing by it, on a grey and cold winter's morning, I listened for the tumults of the past, but all I could hear was the ceaseless sound of the city's motion.

Frenzy might aptly describe the custom, alluded to by Erasmus, of Londoners processing to the cathedral "with a deer's head fixed upon a spear, accompanied with men blowing hunting-horns".[17]

---

16 Milman, 1868, pages 83–84.
17 Arrian, 1831, page 160.

But if the blood of a deer shed before St Paul's represents the wilder reaches of medieval religion, devotion to the saints was the broad stream of the Thames, and in this no saint ranked higher for medieval Londoners than St Thomas Becket. Although Mellitus and Earconwald were the putative patrons of London (along with St Paul, of course, whose tower and spire pierced from the heart of the city seemingly to heaven itself), the murdered archbishop held a unique place in the devotions of Londoners. Becket was a Londoner himself, born on Cheapside, the old Anglo-Saxon artery that had become one of the city's main market streets, and after his martyrdom under the swords of four of Henry II's more suggestible knights, his cult spread to such an extent that four years after his death, Henry had to do public penance at Becket's tomb, walking barefoot into the cathedral at Canterbury and being scourged there by Becket's monks. Such public humiliation for a king indicates just how great were the Church's checks on royal and state power in the high medieval period.

The desire to travel, "to explore strange new worlds", is by no means limited to citizens of the Federation. Medieval Londoners, many of whom were immigrants to the city in the first place, also loved to travel, and pilgrimage was the safest, surest, and most profitable – at least spiritually – form of travel in their day. There were the great pilgrimages, to Jerusalem and to Rome, but far closer at hand and within the means of all but the poorest, there was their very own Thomas, in Canterbury.

> Whan that Aprille, with hise shoures soote,
> The droghte of March hath perced to the roote
> And bathed every veyne in swich licour,
> Of which vertu engendred is the flour...
> Thanne longen folk to goon on pilgrimages
> And palmeres for to seken straunge strondes

To ferne halwes, kowthe in sondry londes;
And specially, from every shires ende
Of Engelond, to Caunturbury they wende,
The hooly blisful martir for the seke
That hem hath holpen, whan that they were seeke.

(When April with his showers sweet with fruit
The drought of March has pierced unto the root
And bathed each vein with liquor that has power
To generate therein and sire the flower...
Then do folk long to go on pilgrimage,
And palmers to go seeking out strange strands,
To distant shrines well known in sundry lands.
And specially from every shire's end
Of England they to Canterbury wend,
The holy blessed martyr there to seek
Who helped them when they lay so ill and weak.)[18]

The traditional start of the pilgrimage was the bridge that symbolized
the city: London Bridge. The bridge was commissioned by Henry
II, Thomas's once friend, in part as expiation for the archbishop's
murder. It was the first permanent stone crossing of the river. And
for the next 650 years city and bridge became synonymous, the
crossing defining London as much as the river had done in previous
centuries. The job was huge, complex, and long – Henry did not live
to see its completion. Nor did the man who designed and built it,
Peter de Colechurch, see it completed in 1209, but his remains did:
they were interred in the chapel, dedicated to Thomas Becket, that
Peter – a priest as well as an architect – placed at the centre of his
great bridge. Old London Bridge was one of the marvels of the age,

---

18 Translation from http://www.canterburytales.org/.

the longest inhabited bridge in Europe, between 800 and 900 feet long and supported by nineteen stone piers, called starlings, sunk into the river bed, each needing regular maintenance. The starlings were not regular, and the river, squeezed between different gaps, churned and frothed into rapids, with the fall from one side of the bridge to the other sometimes, depending on the tide, being greater than a man's height. Thames boatmen soon named the different arches – Long Entry and Gut Lock among them – and shooting the bridge's rapids became an essential part of their trade, although not everyone was willing to take the watery plunge. Cardinal Wolsey normally disembarked above the bridge and met his boat again below.

The chapel to St Thomas on the bridge became the traditional starting point of the Canterbury pilgrimage. It also marked the pilgrims' return. As pilgrimage grew more popular through the Middle Ages, many shrines began to produce souvenir badges, made of lead and pewter, that they sold to pilgrims to mark the successful completion of their pilgrimage. Piers Plowman describes the sight they presented to onlookers:

> Apparelled as a Paynim · in a pilgrim's wise.
> He bare a staff bound · with a broad strip
> In bindweed wise · wound about.
> A bowl and a bag · he bare by his side;
> An hundred ampullas · on his hat set,
> Signs of Sinai · and shells of Galicia,
> Many a cross on his cloak · keys also of Rome
> And the vernicle in front · so that men should know
> And see by his signs what · shrines he had sought.
>
> This folk asked him first · from whence he did come.
>
> "From Sinai," he said · "and from our Lord's sepulchre;
> Bethlehem and Babylon · I have been in both;

> In Armenia, in Ajexandria · and many other places.
> Ye may see by my signs · that sit on my hat
> That I've walked full wide · in wet and in dry,
> And have sought good saints · for my soul's health."[19]

Along with the badges, ampoules were favourite mementos, having the advantage of being sealable, so the pilgrim could fill them with holy water from the shrine. Lots of these badges and ampoules have been found in the Thames near the site of old London Bridge, suggesting that many a pilgrim, having returned from Canterbury or some other pilgrimage site, by way of thanking God for his or her safe return, threw a pilgrimage token into the water from the bridge. The modern compulsion to toss pennies into ponds and fountains taps into the same deep human need to give votive offerings into watery keeping.

Among the pilgrims setting off to Canterbury in Chaucer's tale were a monk and a friar. Monasticism – withdrawal from the world and devotion to a life of prayer – was the paradoxical engine that sustained civilization through the Early Medieval period in Britain, for the communities of monks and nuns that sprang up around the country from the seventh century onwards provided just about the only centres of stability and continuity in a violently uncertain world, where kingdoms rose and fell on the outcomes of a single, bloody skirmish. But, as has ever been the way with religious life, success carried the seed of its own adulteration: the austerity and renunciation of the early monks was gradually vitiated by the gifts of land and gold laid upon the monastic orders through the centuries by a grateful laity, seeking through monkish prayers to ensure their own passage into heaven. Of course, it was no unrelieved decline into laxity with reform movements punctuating the centuries as

---

19 Langland, 1957, page 47.

surely as the wine-bibbing priors of popular protest, yet by the High Middle Ages many of the monastic orders had become synonymous with a life of ease, with only the unflaggingly austere Carthusian order still universally admired for their discipline.

Into this monastic morass, the new mendicant orders of friars – the Dominicans, the Carmelites, the Augustinians and, most of all, the Franciscans – burst like a breaking dam. What distinguished them from the monks was their adjective: despite appearances, a mendicant is not someone unable to darn but a religious who subsists on charity. Unlike the monastic orders, which had accumulated sometimes vast estates to support their houses, the friars depended on alms; neither as individuals nor as organizations were they supposed to acquire property. Their locus of action was different too. Where monks withdrew from the world and supported it invisibly but actively through prayer, the friars plunged into the world, living and travelling among ordinary people, acting as the advance guard for spiritual revival. As such, they were greeted with great popular enthusiasm.

But the world wears down the good. Nor can an organization subsist in the same manner as an individual. So while the mendicant orders strove with the world, they had to accommodate to it as well. For the Franciscans, wedded to Francis's Lady Poverty, this involved the deepest soul-searching. When they first arrived in Britain, not long after Francis's death, the Greyfriars (named after the colour, or lack, of their habits) had adhered strictly to the strictures of their founder. Their houses were placed in the poorest parts of town, from Stinking Lane – which tells its tale in its name – in London, to the decayed town gaol in Cambridge. When an overenthusiastic townsman built a stone dormitory for them in Shrewsbury, the Greyfriars demolished it and replaced it with mud walls. This was the heroic age of the Franciscans, when they walked, whatever the weather and the way, barefooted and bareheaded through the cities of Europe, leaving bloody footprints as their track, and opening the hearts of the new urban poor to their call. But it is the nature of heroic ages not to last. And while Thomas de Eccleston, writing in the thirteenth century, says how the brothers happily drank sour beer and ate bread made from unsieved, coarse grain, by the latter part of the medieval centuries the Franciscans had also settled into something less than the extreme poverty asked of them by their founder – although, in the cycle of decline and renewal characteristic of the religious life, the attenuation of the Franciscan rule provoked the foundation of the independent Observant Friars in 1415. The laity of medieval times was intensely aware of the austerity, or otherwise, of the mendicant and monastic orders, and their prestige in the eyes of Londoners was directly related to how strictly they kept to their vows.

However, while it was clear when the Franciscans fell back from poverty, for an order such as the Dominicans – founded as the order of preachers – matters were not so clear-cut. The Blackfriars landed in England on 5 August 1221, on the very day that their founder, Dominic de Guzman, died, and the thirteen friars who made up the advance party made their way to Oxford, for from its inception the order engaged with the cauldron of ideas stirring in the new universities springing up across Europe. A London priory soon followed, however, and, as men educated and engaged with the latest contemporary ideas, the Dominicans soon became royal favourites, with Blackfriars acting as royal confessors, ambassadors, and envoys. Such was the political muscle of the Dominicans that when they moved from their initial London premises in Holborn to the area between Ludgate Hill and the Thames, Edward I gave permission for the defensive wall of the city of London to be moved to accommodate their house: the only time when London Wall was moved to allow space for new buildings. The great priory they built there was the site of various meetings of parliament and the Privy Council, but most notably it hosted the prelude to its own destruction: the divorce trial of Catherine of Aragon. But more of that in the next chapter. All that remains of the medieval Blackfriars is their name, tacked on to a railway station, although the order of preachers might have enjoyed the fact that the station now bridges the river below.

The fate of the Dominicans' London houses reflects that of almost all the city's medieval establishments: the ceaseless churn – mainly fire, bombs, and builders – that ploughs through the past has destroyed almost everything from that time. If that wasn't enough, as far as London's medieval churches were concerned the Great Rebuilder, Sir Christopher Wren, was the Great Despoiler: only a handful of churches survived the Great Fire of 1666 but that was a case of out of the fire and into rebuilding. Wren remodelled almost all the survivors according to his own tastes: out with gargoyles and stained glass, in with geometry and white light.

The Victorians were no slouches when it came to church restoration either, so what Wren missed, they didn't. The upshot is that there are no medieval churches left in London in their original state: it is a lost time. And maybe that is appropriate, for the era is perhaps further from us today than any other in the city's history, for it proceeded from a unity of belief that the city would not see again.

CHAPTER 4

FIRES OF FAITH

My wife was an impediment to our marriage. Why she was is the subject of this chapter for, 500 years later, the events of the Reformation still cast shadows through history: I was, again, Catholic while she was, for the time being, Church of England. When we filled in the form at my (Catholic) parish church (with a priest who had once been an Anglican vicar) there was a box to tick on "impediments to marriage". Harriet, being Anglican, was an impediment, and the box was duly ticked, to her chagrin until this day. Of course, things have improved between Catholics and Anglicans and this was, really, little more than a box-ticking exercise, but that little tick spoke for centuries of separation, distrust, hatred, and propaganda. And, at least in England, it all began nearly 500 years ago and most of it happened in London. So I thought I had better find out why Harriet was an impediment to our marrying. I started studying the history of the Reformation. And then, I stopped...

The late Douglas Adams – whom I earnestly pray is swapping rueful surprised atheist stories with God as I write – said, "I love deadlines. I love the whooshing noise they make as they go by." I'm the opposite: I love deadlines for setting me to write, while I hate letting them slide past, which I never do. Until this book. This is the first (and I hope only) time I've ever missed a deadline and it was this bloody ("bloody") chapter that made me miss it. I'd finished writing the medieval chapter, I was buzzing along, full of ideas, and then I came to the Reformation and... I stopped. For days, weeks, and even a month or two I could not bring myself to sit down and write, for even now, nearly five centuries afterwards, it hurts too much. Men, women, and children, almost all of them committed to the truth and to God with a depth and passion that I can only dream of, good men and good women, did each other to death over the right way to believe in and worship God.

It is impossible to write about this without facing the capacity for death dealing and destruction that lies at the heart of religion, and thus the possibility that Douglas Adams was, in fact, right. The answer to the question of life, the universe, and everything may really be forty-two, a mundane, divisible, as near-to-ordinary number as any number can be, and the man himself, rather than smiling ruefully at a God revealed to be an even better humourist than him, may now be dust and ashes, unable even to take satisfaction in his own confirmation. There is no better argument for the falsity of Christianity than Christians, and in the Reformation, Christians provided an infinite army of internet atheists with enough ammunition for the ages.

That is why I found this chapter so difficult to write. But we must face the horror and see if, beneath the stripes and lashes and burning flesh, there is anything apart from further levels of horror.

How did this happen? How could the Church – a moral presence once so overwhelming that it could make a king walk barefoot in penance and then, stripped naked, be lashed publicly for his part in murder – how could it be torn apart, destroyed, and remade in a new form by a different king?

So, what happened? For the Crown, as for the Church, the City was vital: whether the old faith or the new prevailed would be decided, above all, in London. I've read book after book on the subject, and the wealth of detail and opposing views threatened to make my brain boil so, in the end, to bring some order to my thoughts I had to reduce the main events of the Reformation down into a few points from which I could work. I suspect it will be no easier for my readers, so here I present my eight-point instant-expert breakdown of the English Reformation, from Henry's divorce to Elizabeth's virginity:

- 1527. Henry VIII asks the pope to annul his marriage to Catherine of Aragon. Catherine has produced six children for the king, but only one, Mary, survived for more than a few weeks. Catherine is now in her early forties, her last pregnancy was nearly ten years earlier, and besides, there is a new girl at court...

- 1529–34. Henry summons what becomes known as the Reformation Parliament. The pope has refused him an annulment so the king decides to place himself at the head of the church in England and grants his own divorce. Henry charges all the clergy in England to accept his new status on pain of death. A series of Acts of Parliament make Henry supreme head of the Church of England.

- 1533. Henry marries the pregnant Anne Boleyn.

- 1536–41. Henry ties the nobility and merchant classes to his Reformation by dissolving the monasteries, selling off their land and possessions to the ruling elite.

- 1538–47. On the ground and in parishes, Protestants – real Protestants that is, who accept Martin Luther's idea that you are saved by faith in Christ alone and for whom Scripture is the source and summit of knowledge – start pushing Henry's

Reformation in directions too radical for a king who, as long as he is in charge of the church, prefers a fairly traditional version of Christianity: a sort of Catholicism light, with Henry as pope. The king pushes back.

- 1547–53. Henry's son, Edward VI, succeeds to the throne as a nine-year-old and, with his chief advisers being determined Protestants, the destruction of the art and symbols of late-medieval Catholicism resumes: rood screens are torn down, statues defaced, stained glass broken, and murals whitewashed.

- 1553–58. Mary, Henry's elder daughter and the child of his first marriage to Catherine of Aragon, becomes queen on Edward's death and attempts to reconstitute Catholicism in England. Mary might, perhaps, have succeeded – if she had lived as long as her successor.

- 1558–1603. Elizabeth, Henry's daughter with Anne Boleyn, becomes queen and enforces a compromise version of Christianity that comes in midway between the traditional Catholicism of Mary and the Protestant radicalism of the reformers, carefully fudging some key doctrinal questions but being just as carefully precise that the monarch shall be supreme governor of the Church of England.

That, in eight bullet points, is the outline of the first part of the English Reformation. In the end, the Reformation played out differently in England as compared to the rest of Europe because of its early adoption by the powers in the land: Henry; two of his three children; and, most importantly in the end, the entire class of the rich and the noble who filled their treasuries and their land portfolios with the expropriated possessions of England's dissolved monasteries and friaries. In a notable example of family fortunes taking precedence over religious recompense, even families that remained stubbornly and devotedly Catholic through Henry's and Edward's reigns had not the slightest inclination to hand back land they had acquired from the old monastic orders during Mary's brief attempt to restore land to its former owners.

Looked at overall, as a historical narrative, I think the English Reformation is best described as a revolt of the aristocracy against the Church, of the rich against the poor, of lawyers against clerics. Throughout Europe, the determining factor for whether countries reformed or not was the decision of kings and princes. England, ever since late-medieval times, had a dissenting "protestant" minority before Protestantism existed: the Lollards. They were followers of John Wycliffe, a fourteenth-century theologian and preacher, who advocated that the Church should divest itself of temporal power: in particular, he argued that the secular power need not answer to the pope, and that authority lay in the Bible. As his teaching came under pressure, he grew more extreme in his views, finally denying the doctrine of transubstantiation. Wycliffe proceeded, with others, to translate the Bible into English. Although his translation was officially suppressed, more copies of his translation survive from that time than of any other text, indicating how widely it was disseminated and how spellbinding the prospect of reading God's word in their own language was to some people.

We live in a visual age, one in which it is difficult to imagine the power of words over people for whom the aural and textual were far more important than the visual. But people would die for words. The Lollards were suppressed after Wycliffe's posthumous condemnation for heresy and, as is the way with persecuted groups, their own doctrines, under pressure, grew more extreme. The first layman to be executed in England for heresy, in 1410, was the Lollard John Badby, who denied, and persisted in denying, that the bread and wine offered during Mass become the body and blood of Christ – and this despite the apparent anxiety of the secular authorities to find Badby a way off the pyre (the crown prince, who became Henry V, tried to get Badby to recant, offering him both life and a lifelong pension should he do so). But Badby burned – in the flesh, as one of the first Lollard martyrs, and in the spirit, with the God madness that infected these first champions of God's word.

For it was a sort of madness. A madness for God and for his truth, as revealed in the Bible, that brooked no compromise. Following the failed Lollard uprising led by Sir John Oldcastle in 1414, when the knight attempted first to kidnap Henry V and then, when that failed, to lead a general uprising with the aim of overthrowing both clergy and nobility, the Lollards formed clandestine groups in England's towns. It took a particular sort of one-eyed religious genius to unite clerics and knights against you, but by taking aim at everyone with power and status in late-medieval England, the Lollards succeeded in doing just that. Those that survived the purge following the failed revolution and Oldcastle's eventual capture and execution went underground, many gravitating towards the one place where there were sufficient people to hide their activities and where were concentrated the printers that could feed their overriding addiction for books: London.

And now, in this, I find a union of belief between myself, a twenty-first-century Catholic, and these late-medieval sectarians. For my first and most profound belief was also in books, in their power and wisdom and, indeed, their beauty. Even those Lollards who were illiterate – which might seem an impossible contradiction but which in fact illustrates the talismanic power ascribed to God's word made visible on paper – loved their books, sometimes unto death. For example, Robert Benet, a wool racker and water carrier (about as humble an occupation as could be found in London), paid over 3s. 4d. for a copy of the Gospels, selling his looms and shears to raise funds for the book, even though he could not read it; instead, he kept his treasure secret and safe in his belt. Or John Harrydance, a bricklayer from Whitechapel, who, despite trying and failing for thirty years to learn how to read, kept his copy of the New Testament always by his side. While Benet and Harrydance might not have been able to read the great words that they carried on their person as intimately as their neighbouring Catholics might carry crucifixes, these truths were presented to them at the Lollards' clandestine gatherings, where the Bible was proclaimed and its message expounded. To receive God's word, aloud or by sight, was the Lollard sacrament, as sacred as the Mass was for their Catholic countrymen.

But in placing God's written word above all else, the Lollards struck at the core of the faith of their neighbours. For while they also placed no value in pilgrimage or prayers for the dead in purgatory – the rope that tied generations living and dead together in Catholic practice – it was in their denial of the real presence of Christ in the sacrament of Mass that they pulled apart the unity of belief that had underlain English society for centuries. And as the political Reformation approached, some among these underground believers, unable to hold silence any longer in the face of what they saw as abominable idolatry, began to speak out.

"I will not give my dogs that bread that some priests doth minister at the altar when they be not in clean life, and also said that thy self could make as good bread as that was and that it was not the body of Our Lord, for it is but bread, for God cannot be both in Heaven and earth."[20] So testified Elizabeth Sampson in 1510. But as long as the Lollards remained an underground movement, without power or influence, they posed little real danger to the contract of beliefs that made up late-medieval society. And

---

20   Brigden, 2014, page 91.

as Lollardy was mainly concentrated among the artisan and lower classes in the city it could largely be ignored by the powers, clerical and secular.

But Henry's determination to place himself at the summit of the church in England meant that, suddenly, all was possible, for whoever had the ear of this most mercurial but implacable of kings had the chance to steer England towards the outcome they desired. Thus the court became a pit of contesting factions, where the penalty for falling from the king's grace was death.

The other great factor in bringing reform to the centre of English life and thought was what was happening elsewhere in Europe. Johannes Gutenberg had invented the first modern printing press around 1439 and, once he had established himself, the technology spread rapidly, with William Caxton establishing the first press in England at Westminster in 1476. With printing in place, the means for a new kind of revolution had been established: a media revolution. For when, in 1517, Martin Luther wrote his Ninety-Five Theses against a travelling Dominican indulgence-seller, Johann Tetzel, the printing press meant that, once his original Latin document was translated into German and published the next year, copies of it spread across Europe almost instantaneously. The printing press magnified the individual voice as a telescope magnified the heavens.

And what Luther said, in prose that was supple and muscular and in his vernacular, was that faith in Christ alone saved the sinner: faith alone, without deeds or actions or virtues or chantries of priests mumbling Masses to perpetuity to release your soul from purgatory. At the cut of his pen, he broke the chain of charity, obligation, and duty that bound the Catholic community to its living and its dead through the offices of priest and monk, saints and prayers and penance. All the doubts and fears and guilt that had built up over 1,500 years of Christian practice and thought were dissolved at a stroke: but only believe, and be saved.

The effect was that of lightning; everything became illumined, and seen, by the light of this one piercing statement. Then, when Luther added his polemic against the papacy, identifying it with the biblical Antichrist, he substantially completed the rhetoric of Reformation. On its positive side, Christians were saved by God's grace alone, through faith alone. On its negative side, the traditions of the Catholic Church, its councils and clergy and the papacy, were traduced, spiritual authority lying only with Scripture, temporal authority with the secular powers.

Although Henry VIII initially set his face against Luther, writing a Defence of the Seven Sacraments that won him the title of *Fidei Defensor* from Pope Leo X, the reformer's ideas were smuggled into the country. The Reformation became a war of pamphlets, of short, quickly produced booklets in the vernacular, cheap and easy to print, and straightforward to reply to. This was the war of ideas played out in front of the public rather than hidden away in the universities and courts.

But first the public had to find these secret texts.

I am a Catholic. I had not thought to find any point of contact with the sacrament-denying Lollards or their Protestant successors. But there was a time when I went searching furtively through obscure London bookshops, looking for texts that no one else knew of, but which seemed to me to contain the secret of the world's religions. This was in the days before the internet, when to find books like this meant browsing shelves in second-hand and occult bookshops, sending off for dog-eared publication lists and, slowly, realizing that there was a shadow second world, where people passed these books among themselves, and met and discussed them. Then, one day, I got off the tube at Hatton Cross and walked a long road, beneath the roar of planes landing and taking off, to knock on a suburban door and enter into another world. That story is for later. But I realized I understood something of the electric, life-changing thrill of finding such secret knowledge.

The old narrative, triumphantly proclaimed by Whiggish historians and apologists for Empire in the eighteenth and nineteenth centuries, was that the English people had risen up against the foreign domination of popes and Church, taking control of a moribund and corrupt clerical structure and taking power back into their own hands. However, the work of historians over the last half-century has shown quite definitively that the Catholicism of England just before the Reformation was far from moribund.

Just how traditional religious beliefs remained in London through the cauldron of the early Reformation is shown by Susan Brigden's analysis of wills in London and the Reformation – for what and to whom a man or woman commends their soul reveals as much as we can know of the hearts of Londoners through this period. The vast majority of wills still invoked the intercession of the Blessed Virgin Mary and called down prayers for the remission of sins and the pains of purgatory; only 6 per cent of wills in the 1530s and 13 per cent in the 1540s were written with a distinctly Protestant language and theology.

But there was one area of festering resentment that the Church had never addressed and which the reformers seized upon. Given the nature of London, it was an appropriate sore: money.

There were a lot of priests in London. There were also a lot of parishes, over a hundred, but these were, on the face of it, overserved: one chronicler counted the clergy as they processed through London in 1535 and reached a figure of 718, and that is leaving aside the monks, friars, and nuns in the city's religious houses. Many served as chaplains. Indeed, Thomas More noted how almost every household in his social circles now included a priest among its members. This many priests cost a lot of money, and Londoners were expected to support them by giving a tenth of their income to their priest. In the countryside, parishioners handed over a tenth of the harvest, so as the harvest went, so went the priest's income: he feasted or starved alongside the people he served. But in London, the tithe was fixed in monetary terms by a bull of Pope Nicholas V, issued in 1453: 3s. 5d. for every £ paid in house rent. Those who owned their houses paid according to the rental value of their home, while parishioners who were not householders, servants, the poor, or apprentices gave a token 8d. over Easter.

Many householders fell into arrears on these payments, a fact attested by the number of wills that included payments for unpaid tithes: while the debts might be delayed in life, they were better paid off at death, lest the soul be called to account for them. Tithe disputes between clergy and parishioners were often bitter and, just as often, came to law: between 1520 and 1546 one-third of London parishes came to court over such matters.

When the eventual success of the Reformation in London is assessed, this factor stands high for why the populace acquiesced in the changes imposed from above.

A significant percentage of priests did not even serve the parishes that paid them. This was not always because the priest was grasping or incompetent: priests had to be provided for while they were being educated. Nor were diocesan clergy, nor chaplains to Crown and nobility, provided with sufficient livings. To make up the shortfall, their masters installed them as the beneficiaries of London parishes, but of course, their time was taken serving court or bishop. Roughly a quarter of London parishes had absent parish priests: in their absence, the care of souls was left to a poorly paid and, usually, worse-educated curate.

It was this wound of resentment against clergy more concerned with Mammon than souls that the reformers salted. Even half a millennium later the vitriol from their pamphlets still burns: "Yea, and they look so narrowly upon their profits that the poor wives must be countable to them for every tenth egg, or else she getteth not her rights at Easter and shall be taken as an heretic."[21] With Henry disposed to bring the church to his heel, and having himself read William Tyndale's *Obedience of a Christian Man*, which asserted that the clergy had usurped unlawfully the power of princes, it was only a matter of time before the dogs were set to feast upon the fat of the church. When Henry set them loose, he chose his target well: the monasteries.

For Londoners, most of the city's monasteries, convents, and friaries had become bywords for indolence, spiritual sloth, and worldly acquisitiveness. So when, in 1534, Thomas Cromwell sent his commissioners to visit the monasteries of England, ostensibly to check their religious practice but in reality to find out how much each was worth, there was little resistance among populace or nobility to the commissioners' report that said, in coded language, that here were riches, ripe for the taking. The reaction of London's religious houses when they were required to swear the Oath of Royal Supremacy, recognizing Henry VIII as head of the church in England, suggests that public opinion was accurate. The priors and abbots signed, the monks and friars were given pensions, and the churches were stripped of all items of value, while relics and holy images were destroyed. What was left, and the land, was sold to the nobility, providing Henry with a huge windfall and, since land was wealth in Tudor times, hugely enriching the aristocratic families that bought out the monastic estates.

But three houses in London refused to accept the king's supremacy. And, embarrassingly for the government, these were the three houses universally acknowledged among Londoners to have kept to the terms of the most stringent religious life: the Observant Franciscans, the Bridgettines and, most severely, the Carthusians of the Charterhouse.

---

21 Brigden, 2014, pages 173–74.

In other, more remote, parts of the country the bones of dead monasteries still lie exposed to the air – to me a voiceless cry to the future against the power of kings; to most visitors picturesque ruins to pose in front of for photographs. But in London, there's nothing left of these old foundations. John Stow, the great London chronicler, writing in 1596 after years of walking the city's streets, still saw the rubble heaps where monastic churches had stood, but London's appetite for space soon swallowed them. There is one exception though: the Charterhouse. I first visited it back in the early 1980s, when my job was delivering and repairing TVs, and one of the retired clergymen who lived there ordered a television from John Lewis. Labouring under the weight of the twentieth century, I entered the square and went into the past.

Cartusia nunquam reformata quia nunquam deformata. "The Charterhouse has never been reformed because it has never been deformed." Pope Pius XI, writing in 1924, reaffirmed the old adage. By then the Carthusians had endured 900 years without slippage. Certainly, in 1535 there was no question of the London Charterhouse being found wanting in religious life. Yet still, and perhaps precisely because of this, Henry required the prior and monks of the Charterhouse to swear to his supremacy.

Carthusians live as hermits in community, each monk having his own cell where he spends most of his time in solitary prayer, the community coming together only for weekly meals. In the city, the throbbing, heaving, bustling city, they bring a great silence. And in that silence they would gladly have remained, having done with all worldly things, but the world, and princes, being what they are, would not, could not, leave them be.

The prior of the Charterhouse was John Houghton. He was born in 1486/7 in Essex and entered the Carthusian order in 1515. Houghton was unanimously elected prior of the London Charterhouse – monks were early democrats – in 1531.

Thomas Cromwell's commissioners first called on the Charterhouse in 1534, requiring Houghton and his monks to swear to the Act of Succession, whereby Henry declared his first marriage to Catherine of Aragon null and void, debarring Mary, daughter of that union, from the throne, while making his marriage to Anne Boleyn valid and thus the children of that marriage next in line to the throne. The Carthusians, and indeed almost all the wives of London, sided with Catherine on this, but when Houghton demurred, pointing out that as solitary monks they had given over dealing with the world, Houghton and his procurator were arrested and sent to the Tower. There, the bishop of London persuaded them that it was possible to square the Act with their consciences so, with reservations, Houghton swore on behalf of his order and was released to the Charterhouse.

But the monks must have known what was to come.

By spring 1535, they knew Henry would have them swear to his supremacy as governor of the church in England, under pain of high treason.

Houghton and his monks prepared themselves through Masses and confession, cleansing their souls for the trial to come. Then, with the priors of the Charterhouses in Axholme and Beauvale, Houghton sought audience with Thomas Cromwell, asking that, as men withdrawn from the world, they be spared the oath-taking. Cromwell put them in the Tower, then interrogated them, along with one of the monks of Syon Abbey, on 26 April. Houghton took notes of the interrogation, sending them to the bishop of Rochester, John Fisher, and his monks in the London Charterhouse.

Under pressure from Cromwell, Houghton and his fellow monks said they were willing to agree to whatever God's law permitted. But, for Cromwell, that was not enough. "I admit no exception. Whether the law of God permits it or no, you shall take the oath without any reserve whatsoever, and you shall observe it too."[22] For Cromwell, the king's agent, there could be no will above that of the monarch.

When Houghton pointed out that what the king asked went against the church's teaching, Cromwell replied, "I care nothing for what the Church has held or taught. I will that you testify by solemn oath that you believe and firmly hold what we propose to you to profess; that the king is Head of the English Church."[23]

Houghton and his fellows were dead, and they knew it.

The trial followed swiftly, on 28/29 April, and when it did not come to the right sentence on two occasions, Cromwell arrived in person to ensure there was no mistake the third time.

Treason. Penalty: to be hung, drawn, disembowelled, decapitated, and quartered.

The sentence was carried out on 4 May 1535 in front of a large crowd at Tyburn. Houghton, as senior, was first, followed by Augustine Webster and Robert Lawrence, priors of Axholme and Beauvale; then Richard Reynolds, monk of Syon Abbey; and a secular priest, John Hale, vicar of Isleworth.

The executioner begged pardon of Houghton, and the prior embraced him. Then, turning to the crowd, Houghton said:

"I call on Almighty God to witness, and I beseech all here present to attest for me on the dreadful danger of judgement, that, being about to die in public, I declare that I have refused to comply with the will of His Majesty the King, not from obstinacy, malice, or a rebellious spirit, but solely for fear of offending the Supreme Majesty of God. Our Holy Mother the Church has decreed and enjoined otherwise than the king and Parliament have decreed. I am therefore bound in conscience,

---

22   Quoted in Hendriks, 1928, page 18.
23   Quoted in Hendriks, 1928, page 20.

and am ready and willing to suffer every kind of torture, rather than deny a doctrine of the Church. Pray for me, and have mercy on my brethren, of whom I have been the unworthy Prior."[24]

Houghton was hanged, but only briefly, so he was still fully conscious when cut down. Then the executioner disembowelled him. Houghton's last words, as the executioner reached to rip the heart from his body, were, "Good Jesu, what will ye do with my heart?" Then he was decapitated and his body quartered. Houghton's head went onto London Bridge; one of his arms was nailed, in warning, to the door of the London Charterhouse.

His four fellows followed him as martyrs.

The monks of the Charterhouse ignored the warning. Five died as their prior did, ten others were starved to death in Newgate prison.

Many others would die as martyrs during the Reformation, Catholic and Protestant, but amid the welter of blood shed in the name of religion, one fact shines out: Houghton and his companions, Latimer, Ridley, and Cranmer for the Protestants, died as true martyrs; that is, as ones faithful unto death and giving witness to the truth (as they saw it) by their deaths. This is the true meaning of the red crown of martyrdom, and it is well, when its meaning is being perverted today, that we remember that.

But what is notable is that, other than these few, when the clergy of England were faced with the choice of swearing to their king or taking death in faith for their father in Rome, they chose life. Swing conscience how they might, the vast majority of the Catholic clergy in England put on the robes of discretion rather than the crown of martyrdom. If the clergy of England had refused, as a body, to accept the royal supremacy, maybe matters would have turned out differently, although Henry would have shed much blood at such

---

24 Quoted in Hendriks, 1889, pages 152–53.

defiance. But with Thomas More, their main advocate at court, also gone, there was no stomach for defiance among the majority of the clergy – most chose the apparent wisdom of waiting and prayer, that these evil days might pass.

Thomas More, when he accepted the Chancellery from Henry VIII in 1529, knew well that he dined with a man of no more conscience than a lion, and as implacable in his desires. "If my head would win him a castle in France, it should not fail to go," More said to his son-in-law.[25]

It didn't win him a castle in France, but it did quiet the conscience of the king in the matter of his remarriage.

More's reputation as a man of intelligence, honour, and integrity was Europe-wide. He and Erasmus, the most famous of the Christian Humanist scholars who prepared the way for Renaissance (by design) and Reformation (by accident), were friends for thirty-five years; indeed, Erasmus wrote *Praise of Folly* while staying with More in England. Its Latin title (*Moriae Encomium*) can also be read as "in praise of More" – the double meaning was intentional.

More had not pursued the king's friendship – quite the opposite. But Henry took to calling unexpectedly at More's house – one can only imagine the kitchen panic when the king decided to stay for dinner – and More, a member of parliament and, latterly, its Speaker, could not remain outside the royal orbit any longer; he became the Chancellor in 1529.

But when Henry asserted his supremacy over the Church, More found he could no longer serve the king. In 1532, pleading ill health, he asked to be relieved of office, and he was. However, the factions vying for Henry's favour all knew well the fickleness of the king: a fallen favourite could not be left to return to favour, but had to be destroyed entirely.

---

25 Quoted in Chalmers, 1815, page 366.

In 1533, Thomas More was called to trial for refusing to take the Oath of Supremacy, declaring Henry governor of the church in England, with the power to declare the church's doctrine – a power that even unsettled Luther. His chief inquisitor was Thomas Cromwell, the man who had supplanted him as Henry's key counsellor. The jury was composed of More's enemies: Cromwell, the new Chancellor, and the father, brother, and uncle of the king's new wife; even so, they could find nothing on which to condemn him – for More held silence, refusing either to affirm or deny his acceptance of the king's supremacy over the church – until Richard Rich, the solicitor general at the time, testified that in private conversation More had told him the king could not be the true head of the church.

Taken by surprise, More still responded with the wit of his long years of legal training:

> In good Faith, Mr. *Rich,* I am more concerned for your Perjury, than my own Danger; and I must tell you, that neither my self nor any body else to my knowledge, ever took you to be a Man of such Reputation, that I or any other would have any thing to do with you in a Matter of Importance. You know that I have been acquainted with your manner of Life and Conversation long time, even from your Youth to the present Juncture, for we lived in the same Parish; and you very well know, I am sorry I am forced to speak it, you always lay under the Odium of a very lying Tongue, of a great Gamester, and of no good Name and Character either there or in the *Temple,* where you was educated. Can it therefore seem likely to your Lordships, that I should in so weighty an Affair as this, act so unadvisedly, as to trust Mr. *Rich.*[26]

---

26 Source: http://law2.umkc.edu/faculty/projects/ftrials/more/moretrialreport.html.

The jury took fifteen minutes to find him guilty. The sentence was to be hanged, drawn, and quartered; Henry commuted that to decapitation.

Thomas More was executed on 6 July 1535. As he prepared to ascend the scaffold, he told the executioner, "Pray, Sir, see me safe up; and as to my coming down, let me shift for myself."[27] As he stood upon the scaffold, More told the crowd, "I die the King's good servant, and God's first."[28] Then, laying his head upon the block, the executioner struck it off with a single stroke.

But the king he served was turning from the golden hope of his youth to the murderous favouritism of his maturity. And nowhere was that favour more tragically bestowed than upon the woman who was the cause of More's death: Anne Boleyn.

For where More had used the short years of his chancellorship in a furious attempt to root heresy from the realm, it had already been implanted in the very bed of the king, for Boleyn herself was won to the Gospel.

The old heresy of the Lollards, confined largely to the artisan classes and shorn of political strength by its history of rebellion, could never have been other than a minor sect. But the new faith of the evangelicals won converts through all levels of society, its promise of salvation through faith alone cutting through the slow encrustation of medieval devotional practices like a saw through rotten wood. Rather than having, as some saw, to achieve salvation through the mediation of a church that, in its personal embodiment, was all too often flawed, faith, and faith alone, expressed in and through the innermost room of the heart, was not just the key to salvation but salvation itself. But believe, and

---

27 Source: http://law2.umkc.edu/faculty/projects/ftrials/more/
moretrialreport.html.
28 Seemingly a translation of a French account of his execution; see:
http://www.thomasmorestudies.org/quotes_1.html.

you will be saved. For some people, particularly those prone to scrupulosity, the simplicity of this message must have cut to the core. And Anne was one of them.

The woman who was to be queen had spent most of her childhood and her teenage years at the great courts of Europe as maid of honour to queens and, while there, she seems to have developed the commitment to the vernacular Gospel and reform that was to make her short period of influence the most transformative in English history.

By 1522, when Anne returned to England, Catherine was thirty-six. Her last pregnancy had been four years before and there would be no more. Anne was stylish and intelligent, with a fierce humour that made her a match for the king, and he was soon pursuing her, as he had pursued her elder sister, Mary. But Anne was not satisfied to be a royal mistress: she would be queen if Henry would have her in his bed. In a book of hours, Henry wrote:

> I am yours
> Henry R forever.

In reply Anne wrote:

> By daily proof you shall me find
> To be to you both loving and kind.

This message was written beneath a picture of the annunciation, when the Archangel Gabriel announced to Mary that she would bring forth a son. Anne was making Henry a promise. In the end, it was her failure to keep this promise that cost her her life.

But that was later. Anne was crowned queen on 1 June 1533, although her influence had been considerable for the previous four years. She was already pregnant. As queen, Anne promoted reform, placing men committed to the Gospel in positions of power and working to protect others. In this stratagem, she had an ally, and a vital one, in the new Thomas who had taken the place of Thomas More as her husband's most important adviser: Thomas Cromwell.

During his youth, spent travelling – obscurely in the eyes of history – around Europe, Cromwell had learned by heart the New Testament. Of humble stock, he knew full well his advancement at court lay solely in the king's power, and as such he sought always to see that Henry's will be done; although, where possible, that will might be shaped to advance the other cause to which he was committed alongside his own power: that of the Gospel. Indeed, since every man is the hero of his own story, I am sure that Cromwell told himself – and he might even have believed – that he sought power for the sake of advancing the Gospel and not for his own aggrandizement. So the present evil done is excused for the future good it will allow. By such easy, small steps a good man becomes, in time, a monster.

With the queen and the king's chief adviser both committed to the Gospel, the evangelicals had in place vital protection during these early, crucial years, when their numbers were still few and their penetration of society only patchy. If Henry had turned to stamping out heresy with the implacability he brought to his other wishes, there is little doubt that the new religion would have been burned from England before it ever had a chance to take root. But, instead, the Reformation twisted and reacted through the rest of his reign, as one faction after the other gained the king's ear, and Henry's own theological meanderings dictated and halted change.

A king changeable in his theological opinions was malleable of heart too. Having divorced a queen for Anne, and having split the Church for Anne, Henry grew weary of her. A fiery spirit rouses to pursuit but it may less easily be lived with, particularly when the first issue of the gamble upon which Henry had risked all was a girl. The king had convinced himself that his failure to produce an heir with Catherine was due to God's displeasure at his having married his brother's betrothed. Now, when Anne brought forth as firstborn a daughter – despite all the predictions of the court astrologers (and this was a time when those claiming arcane knowledge might gain entrance into the highest circles) – the self-righteous certainty of doing what was right in God's eyes that had sustained Henry through his divorce began to crumple. If God was on his side, then Anne should have borne him his longed-for son and heir.

For her part, Anne had brought into the highest circles of the court her own men, including her brother, Lord Rochford. They advanced the cause to which the queen herself was committed but, being her men, they were vulnerable should she fall, as they well knew. But, in the end, the queen's enemies were to use her men to bring her down.

Catherine of Aragon died on 7 January 1536. When news reached the court, Henry and Anne appeared, dressed both in yellow, and they danced. Anne was pregnant, while Catherine, who had signed her last letter to Henry "Katharine the Queen", was gone and thus, by any lights, queen no longer. The king, rubbing salt into her demise, had her buried as dowager Princess of Wales and prevented Mary from attending her mother's funeral.

Less than three weeks later, Anne miscarried the boy child she was carrying. God, it must have seemed to Henry, had turned his face from him. For his part, the king turned his face from Anne to Jane Seymour, whom the contending faction at court presented to him as the antithesis of his fierce queen.

As the contending factions fought by whisper and rumour and honeyed smile, Cromwell realized that, if he was identified with Anne, then he would be lost – and the Gospel cause too – if she fell. By this time he must have thought the queen wild and fey, for she sanctioned her almoner, John Skip, to preach on

2 April 1536, Passion Sunday itself, on how King Solomon, once so wise, became a fool for lust and how Queen Esther had sought to persuade her king not to follow the advice of his evil counsellor, Haman. There was only one man the court would think on when hearing such preaching: Thomas Cromwell, the man who dangled the seemingly unlimited wealth of England's monasteries in front of Henry's cash-strapped eyes. The Gospellers were serious in their commitment to using such money for the relief of the poor; Henry was even more serious in his quest for martial glory. But war did not come cheap. What Anne and her faction would have given to the poor and to establish the Gospel, Thomas promised to the king.

For the greater good, such evil is done. Thomas Cromwell, so committed to the Gospel that he had imprinted it upon his mind and in his heart, joined with Anne's enemies – with the faction that most bitterly opposed the vision of religion he himself sought – that he might bring the queen down rather than share in her ruin. Thus he might be saved and, with his saving, the Gospel might still have voice in the king's chamber.

As Lord Thomas Howard, Anne's uncle, remarked, the king was not inclined "to hold in affection any person he had cast from him that formerly he had loved,"[29] but this was not simply a matter of casting aside a mistress: this was the queen for whom Henry had broken the Church. Her downfall must needs be as absolute as her rising.

Cromwell moved fast. On 30 April a court musician was arrested and put to torture. He confessed to adultery with Anne and implicated others of higher standing, including Anne's own brother, George, to whom she had complained that the king had "neither talent nor vigour" in bed. George had let the aspersion

---

29 Quoted in Brigden, 2000.

slip and, for a king of Henry's overweening vanity – think on the size of Henry's armoured codpiece, now on display at the Tower of London – such an insult was fatal. Anne was arrested on 2 May 1536 and put in the Tower.

The adultery of a queen was treason. The men accused of it, though most probably innocent, were executed on 17 May. Anne followed them two days later. All accounts agree on her bravery when faced with execution and even as she stood upon the scaffold her quicksilver mind stopped any bitter words against the husband and king who was about to murder her, lest Henry, ever implacable, use them against her daughter.

The king was not there to see her die, but Cromwell was.

The next day, Henry was betrothed to Jane Seymour.

Ten days later, they married.

For her part, Seymour was generous to the children of Henry's first two marriages, in particular trying to convince Henry to restore Mary to the line of succession – after any children that she bore, naturally.

But Jane's first task was to produce a son and heir. On 12 October 1537 she gave birth to a son and he lived. But the boy was the death of her. Jane Seymour died on 24 October 1537. Ten years later, when Henry himself died, he was buried beside her.

But there would be more deaths and more burnings before Henry's end. The Gospellers, with Cromwell still holding his place in the king's counsels, moved to banish superstition and idolatry from the nation. In place of images and relics, there would be the word; but the first could not be allowed to exist, lest they pollute the purity of Scripture. Commissioners of religious purity were dispatched around the country to root out pictures and relics and shrines, and to bring them to London for burning. An innocent faith that had been sustained by such physical supports as the Rood of Grace of Boxley Abbey was defamed and desecrated, local parishioners looking on helplessly as the king's commissioners ripped the objects of veneration from their churches. Such was the iconoclastic fury that, when the holy images and relics were brought for burning, the destroyers taunted the statues and images and pathetic relics to defend themselves from the flames.

In place of these, the Gospellers had the Bible. At the same time as the age-old relics were gathered and destroyed, an English-language Bible was placed in every church. With the breaking of the old, everything now seemed possible. Evangelical zealots defamed the Mass, dissent and division spread through the land. For his part, knowing that the king would not tolerate such religious extremes, Thomas Cromwell tried to keep reports of the unrest from reaching the king, but in the swirling pit of rumour and news that was the Henrician court, even Cromwell could not keep the king from hearing what was happening in what was now his church.

Dressed all in white, Henry himself tried a Gospeller for denying the real presence of Christ in the Eucharist and, finding the man guilty, had him burned. This was his church and the king was not and never would be a Gospeller. In the face of the enthusiasm of the evangelicals, the Act of Six Articles was passed in 1539, making the penalty for denial of transubstantiation death by burning; once found guilty, not even recantation could save the accused from the flames. The act had all the implacability of the king and, when some Gospellers defied it, they increased the pressure on their erstwhile protector, Thomas Cromwell.

As it is a truth universally acknowledged that a king in possession of a kingdom must be in want of a queen, Cromwell had set to work to find a bride for Henry. The king was still mourning. Henry, although never a slight man, only became the bloated figure known to history after Jane's death – his appetites, physical, moral, and spiritual, revealed in his body. To that end, Cromwell engineered Henry's marriage to Anne of Cleves in January 1540, hoping to cement an alliance with those princes in Germany who had aligned themselves to the Lutheran cause. Unfortunately for Cromwell, Henry found her physically repellent: he could "never in her company be provoked and steered to know her carnally"[30]. The marriage was annulled, on the grounds of non-consummation – an annulment that Anne did not oppose – and Cromwell was confined to the Tower.

The many men and women whose deaths Cromwell had engineered over the decade of his power had met death with extraordinary bravery. From the Tower, Cromwell wrote to Henry, pleading for his life in the most unctuous terms:

> If I have not, to the uttermost of my remembrance, said the truth, and the whole truth in this matter, God never help me... beseeching Almighty God... so he now will vouchsafe to counsel you, preserve you, maintain you, remedy you, relieve and defend you, as may be most to your honour, wealth, prosperity, health and comfort of your heart's desire. For the which, and for the long life and prosperous reign of your most royal Majesty, I shall during my life, and while I am here, pray to Almighty God, that he of his most abundant goodness will help, aid and comfort you, and after your continuance of Nestor's years, that the most noble imp, the Prince's Grace, your most dear son, may succeed you to reign long, prosperously, felicitously to God's pleasure: beseeching most humbly your Grace to pardon this my rude writing, and to consider that I am a most woeful prisoner, ready to take the death, when it shall please God and your Majesty; and yet the frail flesh inciteth me continually to call to your Grace for mercy and pardon for mine offences; and thus Christ save, preserve and keep you. Written at the Tower this

---

30   Fraser, 2007.

Wednesday, the last of June, with the heavy heart and trembling hand of your Highness's most heavy and most miserable prisoner and poor slave,

Thomas Cromwell
Most gracious Prince, I cry for mercy, mercy, mercy![31]

Cromwell might as well have asked mercy of a lion, yet still he begged. Henry heard him not, and his death, when it came on 28 July 1540, was one of the most bungled in Tudor history, a cack-handed executioner taking three strikes of the axe to finally detach Cromwell's head and send him to judgement.

All Cromwell's political power and patronage of reformers was based on his being able to find means to achieve Henry's will. Mrs Thatcher said of one of her ministers, "Others bring me problems, David brings me solutions." Cromwell was such an operator in Henry's court, but when his solution failed, he fell.

Henry himself had seven more years of life ahead of him. He would be adulterously betrayed by his next wife, Catherine Howard, and, naturally, he had her executed too. The most handsome prince in Christendom became so bloated that he needed help to move, and his body became covered with boils. Death, when it came, took its time; for nine days Henry lay abed, unable to move, the abscesses in his legs bursting, the king himself kept in ignorance that death stalked him for, by his own statute, to prophesy the death of the king was treason.

Finally, Sir Anthony Denny, a Gentleman of the Privy Chamber, told Henry that "in man's judgement you are not likely to live". A few hours later the king died.

Ten years before, with their abbey and the intricate web of prayer and obligation and oath that bound together Catholic

---

31   Burnet, 1816, page 301.

England lying in ruins, the monks of St Albans Abbey had asked how all had come to nothing.

"The king hath done it on his high power," they answered.

They were right.

Through the cataclysmic events of Henry's reign the fear of a rising, by the general population that the reformers knew only too well was still attached to the old ways, lay under the savagery of the punishments meted to those who spoke against the king and his will. Nowhere were there more people than in London; nowhere was the fear of popular rising greater and yet, and yet... nothing. The people of London did not rise to defend monks or abbeys, nor yet their rood screens and relics. When the north rose, in the Pilgrimage of Grace, London seethed with rumour but nothing more. Indeed, the single greatest outbreak of popular anger in the capital was directed not against Henry but against Anne, who was trapped by a mob of thousands of women in a house by the river, only managing to escape by boat.

The majority of Londoners, as with their clergy, had kept their heads low through Henry's reign. The analysis of wills indicates that the majority still believed in much of the old way, asking for the intercession of the Blessed Virgin Mary and the saints, but an increasing minority cast wills in explicitly evangelical terms. So far had such thought spread that when one of a group of neighbours drinking in the Bell tavern, Aldgate, said, "Masters, let us make our reckoning that we may go to church and hear our High Mass," another answered, "Tarry," and, taking bread, raised it, then signed the cross over a cup of wine before raising it too. "Have ye not heard Mass now?" The man who thus mocked the Mass was Giles Harrison, the king's ale brewer and one of the richest men in London.

Could such changes be reversed? That was what evangelicals feared and Catholics hoped. The king was dead; long live the king.

Edward was not yet ten. A child, to the nation he was a blank slate upon which hopes and fears might be painted. But the kingdom and the city he inherited had been fundamentally altered. The holy stones that knitted London into the kingdom of heaven and the communion of the dead, the priories and abbeys and friaries, were despoiled, their roofs ripped off, leaving dead stone to the elements and their carcases to be picked over by the grandees who governed in Edward's stead until he came of age. John Stow, first chronicler of London, looked on the vandalism with despair.

But others saw this new reign as the chance to bring in, for good and all, the pure, reformed religion of which they dreamed. London's parishes were each power centres, some driving on reform, some pulling back to the old ways. At St Martin Ironmonger Lane, the rood screen was torn down, the statues removed, and the walls washed pure, new white. "Thou shalt make no graven images, lest thou worship them." So the rector wrote upon the white, and other messages from Scripture. With a boy king and, until he married and produced a child, the next in line to the throne being the defiantly Catholic daughter of Catherine of Aragon, all stood yet in balance. Or so it must have seemed.

In truth, the Tudor religious settlement had been pretty well reached by the end of Henry's reign, although nobody knew it yet. The religious radicals surrounding the boy king – and the boy himself, no whit less radical – would try to push reform further; Mary, defining herself and defined by her faithfulness to her mother and the old order, attempted to burn away the new; but both were defined, in the end, by the briefness of their reigns. What, in the end, decided the religion of London and England was longevity: Henry reigned for thirty-eight years, Edward VI for six years, Mary for five, and Elizabeth for forty-four years. In a country where there were many more people under twenty-five than over forty-five, even by the time Mary came to the throne the proportion of the population who remembered the old religious order was small; by the end of Elizabeth's rule, it had almost vanished.

Also, by the end of Elizabeth's reign one-half of the argument was over: England was no longer a Catholic country. The people that had for centuries held a special reverence for the office of Peter, with Anglo-Saxon monarchs raised on the tale of how Pope Gregory the Great had sent his great mission to their country at the end of the world, had rejected the Petrine office. England and the English were to be a new people, a chosen people, singled out by reason of geography and faith for a singular mission. What remained to be settled was what sort of a Protestant country England was to become. That argument was to be settled by civil war, and the reaction to that war.

But now, looking back over the Tudor era from a life in which my wife became an obstacle to our marriage and I found myself governor at a Church of England school, what can I say? That the most fraught period in English history can best be understood as the reactions of Henry's traumatized children to the monstrous shadow he cast over them – and Henry himself as the vainglorious rebellion of a man whose self-worth came to be fundamentally based on fear. In this respect, Henry was a true Renaissance prince – Machiavelli would have been proud.

Edward, the longed-for son, bore the fewest scars from his upbringing; if he had lived, his reign would no doubt have been secure and, as a prince committed to the Gospel, he would have completed the reformation of religion.

Mary. Poor, bloody Mary. Forced from the succession, her mother and her own legitimacy denied, is it any wonder that she clung with all the force of her not inconsiderable courage to the religion of her childhood, when all must have been secure? But then, and this must be faced, when the longed-for child proved but a phantom of her hope, she tried to burn the country back to the old ways, as if the blindness of God in his heaven could be pierced by the smoke of heretics.

Burning human flesh has a peculiar, utterly distinctive sweet smell. Nothing else smells like it and, once smelled, it is never forgotten. I know, from smelling my own flesh burn beneath a lighted cigarette[32] (you know how it goes; you're young, you're stupid, depressed and daring, and wanting something to make you feel alive, so, well, you stub out a cigarette on your arm. And then another. And another).

It hung, thick and sweet, in the alleys and streets of London. The Protestants had their martyrs, as the Catholics had theirs, and all agreed that there was one Church and one Faith, but all were sure it was theirs.

For Londoners in particular, both clergy and laypeople, the choice lay between partisanship or a careful navigation of the conflicting streams of royal policy. Most chose the latter, keeping the secrets of their faith in their hearts and their observance in line with what was required of them. Where the rulers of France long knew to fear the Parisian mob, in London, whose crowds were just as feared, the people did not rise. They adapted, they trimmed and adjusted and saw the zealots burn and the "traitors" dismembered, and they remembered the dreadful sanctions of the Tudor state.

But as the wars of religion spread through Europe, running from 1524 to the end of the Thirty Years' War in 1648, and the Protestant cause waxed and waned, London, as the capital of the

---

32 And from the cremated remains of some of the victims of Dennis Nilsen, the serial killer. I used to drive the streets of north and west London every day throughout the late 1970s, 1980s, and 1990s. One of my main cut throughs was Melrose Avenue, NW10. Nilsen lived at 195 Melrose Avenue and killed at least nine men there, burning their remains in the garden behind his flat. Although he sought to conceal the smell by putting a tyre on top of the pyre, I remember the sickly burning smell that often permeated the air as I drove along the road, never realizing its source.

greatest European state to have declared against Rome, became a refuge for many reformers fleeing the continent. The religious air was slowly changing. Under Elizabeth, it became clear that the Catholics had lost the battle against the Reformation: England was now a Protestant country; indeed, a country increasingly defined by its Protestantism. But the Reformation had pulled apart... well, everything. And through the cracks crawled all sorts of ideas that it had not even been possible to think in the old medieval world.

PART II: NEW WAYS

CHAPTER 5

GODNAROK

The reformers had cracked the world apart. They had broken it for God, but a broken world, for whatever reason it has been broken, is unified no longer. With the old medieval unity of vision lost, all manner of ideas were suddenly possible. Things that had once been, quite simply, inconceivable were now swimming into imaginative reach. The spiritual history of London after the Reformation is the history of these previously undreamed ideas. So, rather than continuing to march through the centuries, in this second part of the book I will switch to examining each of these master ideas in turn. The first idea was the one that would have been most unimaginable to the medieval mind: Godnarok – the twilight of God.

The 27 June 1971 is a day chiefly remarkable for its lack of history. Searching for anything significant that happened, I'm reduced to the closure of *You're a Good Man, Charlie Brown* at the John Golden Theatre on Broadway and another ending: the doors shutting on Fillmore East, the rock venue in New York that became known, apparently, as "the church of rock 'n' roll". But while that Sunday passed unnoticed in the wider world, it was significant for me, for it was the day I finally became a proper, honest-without-God atheist.

That may not have been quite the desired outcome, as 27 June 1971 was also the day of my first Holy Communion. Oh, I'd been toying with disbelief for two or three years by then, first threatening God with withholding my faith whenever I needed a goal in a crunch playground football match ("Let us win and I'll definitely believe in you"), moving to ultimatums ("I'll only believe in you if we score in the next two minutes") and, finally, threats ("You'd better let us win or I definitely won't believe in you"), but God, for his part, had always come through: we'd won all those matches. So while the books I revered might suggest that the world could get on perfectly well without God – evolution and science had shuffled him out of the picture – when it came down to the nitty-gritty of a child's faith, God had been doing the deity work: he'd answered my prayers. So I was prepared to give him the benefit of my doubt.

Besides, there was a big event coming up, when I finally would get to meet God, in the most intimate and personal way imaginable: by eating him. That was what Sister Paula told us. She was the head teacher of my primary school and, in the league table of scary nuns, occupied a mid-ranking spot, high above such failures of fright as Sister Maureen, who actually made you feel as if the sun had come out whenever she smiled, but well below out-and-out monsters such as Sister Sheila, who taught me in secondary school and who managed to terrify generations of tough Islington teenaged boys. She was herself outdone when, in a move to show that God was not above playing jokes on his own religious devotees, she had to change her original name in religion. As a result of the huge success of a 1974 film, her original name became untenable: Sister Emmanuelle had acquired other connotations apart from "God is with us".

So, the day came. All the girls from my primary school class were dressed up in white and having their photos taken looking angelic – and, in truth, most of them were. While the 1960s may have swung, in my immigrant suburb of north London the mores of a decade earlier largely prevailed: I went through my entire primary school life until eleven without hearing any swear word worse than "bloody" and, not realizing that it was a mild expletive, had my mouth washed out with soap by my mother when I used it myself at home. I suppose all us boys were dressed up too, although this was a time when cameras were still rare, so I cannot say if our trousers were flared, our lapels broad, and our ties so psychedelic they might induce flashback in acid heads in the congregation. I have no memory of any of this. What I was interested in was God.

I'd already uncovered the truth about Father Christmas – he was, in fact, not portly, white haired, white, and bearded, but brown skinned, moustached, and my dad – and scientists, as they said in books, had dug up dinosaurs, conspicuously absent from the Bible, and shown that it took rather longer than six days to make the world. The angel light that lights babies into the world and, for some children, continues to illuminate what they see into their childhood, had gone out early for me: the world was prosaic, a puzzle to be uncovered rather than a wonder to be discovered. Each time I re-read my favourite book, *The Wind in the Willows*, I always skipped past the haunted halfway chapter, "The Piper at the Gates of Dawn", in favour of the adventures of Mole, Ratty, Badger, and Mr Toad. I must have been a boring child!

But one uncertainty still intruded into my controlled little world, and a big one at that. However, there was a time and date when it would all become clear and, come the big day, I still remember the excitement as we walked up Highgate Hill to church. Of a blessing, since my first Holy Communion programme was done in conjunction with my school, it was to take place in St Joseph's rather than St Gabriel's, the concrete faith abattoir that was our parish church. St Joseph's, on the other hand, is something of a London landmark, its green great dome visible from miles around.

The church, from the outside, particularly when climbing the hill, seems like some sort of monastic fortress, surmounted with slightly incongruous green domes, but within it's all marble, statues, candles, and baldacchino: a Catholic fantasy church.

The building of it must have seemed a fantasy too, back in 1849, when a Fr Ivers rented a room in Highgate, at 17 High Street, to celebrate Mass, only for the presence of papists to bring rioters onto the streets of Highgate (nowadays, the only thing likely to bring protestors out on the street there would be McDonald's trying to buy its way into the area). But nine years later, when the site of what was once the Old Black Dog pub was auctioned, Fr Ignatius Spencer (yes, he was from that Spencer family, which a century later produced Princess Diana), a convert to Catholicism, put in the winning bid. The first church soon proved too small for a Catholic population being swelled by the Irish workmen coming over to build the Victorian railways, many of whom settled in the network of terraced streets around Archway, near the new railway lines where many of them worked. So in 1889 a new church, the one we see now, was built on the site. This was an era of Catholic confidence: the Catholic Emancipation Act was passed in 1829 and Fr Spencer was himself a product of and instrumental in that self-confidence: that a scion of such an aristocratic family should convert to Catholicism suggested much had changed in the previous half-century.

The faith St Joseph's had proclaimed by so grand an architectural statement at the close of the nineteenth century had grown somewhat flat by the end of the 1960s. The excitement of the Second Vatican Council had trailed away into the liturgical and clerical confusion of the 1970s (it's notable that the majority of the abuser priests who were to prey on children later had their formation during this time[33]),

33 The causes of the sex-abuse crisis in the Church were varied and are beyond the scope of this book, but one factor was the change of outlook that

but I knew nothing of that. I had grown up in the new church; all I knew was Mass in the vernacular and priests, generally sporting hideous polyester vestments, facing us in the congregation. But I lived in an Irish/Italian Catholic milieu: first Holy Communion was a big deal. And I was tremulous with excitement, waiting in line, hands in the prayer position, then kneeling at the altar rail (most Catholic churches still asked people to kneel to receive Communion then), staring at the open tabernacle behind the altar, its polished interior glowing like a glimpse of heaven, and glancing down the line as the priest, with solemn altar server, approached, placing the flat white discs on proffered pink tongues.

Then it was my turn.

"The body of Christ."

And there he was, on my tongue. I closed my mouth. The Host stuck to the suddenly dry roof of my mouth.

Should I bite it?

Should I chew God?

I was walking back to my pew, hands back in the prayer position, and then I knelt again.

"Taste and see that the Lord is good," the choir was singing.

The Lord tasted... dry. And tasteless. He wasn't even bread. More like a cream cracker.

I swallowed.

Was that it?

I looked up. Heaven had not opened. God had not spoken.

---

accompanied the Second Vatican Council. Throwing open the windows to the world meant also that the old strictures and sanctions became less tangible. Mark 9:42 ("If anyone causes one of these little ones – those who believe in me – to stumble, it would be better for them if a large millstone were hung around their neck and they were thrown into the sea" [NIV]) should have served as warning enough. But when everything becomes possible, then nothing is certain, and the old conviction that punishment must follow sin was lost amid the general cultural shift towards a psychologizing of behaviour.

Was that really it?

I glanced sidelong, saw the other children beside me, heads bowed in prescribed prayer positions, mouths moving.

Words.

They were just words, mumbled to the dark.

I had given God his last chance and he had failed. Worse, he had disappointed me.

I left church an atheist in mind and heart.

At the heart of much modern atheism seems to me to lie a hurt disappointment: a question has been posed, an answer sought, and the only response has been silence. But if God had disappointed me, he must have really pissed off Christopher Marlowe.

> Philosophy is odious and obscure.
> Both law and physic are for petty wits.
> Divinity is basest of the three,
> Unpleasant, harsh, contemptible and vile...[34]

Shakespeare wrote of old crones upon a blasted heath, a magic of the past, but the subtlest of all playwrights had heard the fate of his contemporary, the man who wrote magic into the circles of wealth and privilege where it was finding new practitioners, and Shakespeare had sense enough to call no curses down upon his own head. But his friend and rival, the man who drew the devil from hell and placed him upon the Elizabethan stage, played no temporizing games and called down the heavens and declared the old terrors empty:

> Think'st thou that Faustus is so fond to imagine
> That after this life there is any pain?
> Tush, these are trifles and old wives' tales.[35]

---

34 *Doctor Faustus*, Marlowe, 1969, page 269.
35 *Doctor Faustus*, Marlowe, 1969, page 283.

Christopher Marlowe was the first modern metropolitan. And, as is proper for a metropolitan, he was not born in London, but in Kent, and later educated at Cambridge. But his milieu, in his short life, was the violent, shifting world of Elizabethan drama and espionage, and most of that was played out in the new theatres and old taverns of London. The absolute facts of his life are almost as scanty as those of his contemporary, and the web of rumour that surrounds him is every bit as sticky as that around Shakespeare (one theory even equates the two, positing that Marlowe faked his own death and reinvented himself as another playwright). Most likely a Catholic once himself, Marlowe turned double agent and went abroad, to Rheims, to act as agent provocateur against the Catholic exiles there; then, in London, he wrote shifting plays of damnation and desire: *The Jew of Malta* begins with Machevill announcing, "I count religion but a childish toy,/And hold there is no sin but ignorance." The Jewish, Christian, and Muslim protagonists then all bid to outdo each other in venality, concupiscence, and savagery.

The only surprise is that Marlowe lived so long. He died on 30 May 1593, stabbed to death by one Ingram Frizer. Frizer, and two other men present, had all been agents of Elizabeth's spymasters. The coroner's account, that Marlowe and Frizer quarrelled over the bill ("the Reckoning") so violently that Marlowe attacked Frizer who killed Marlowe in self-defence, is possible – this was a time of prickly tempers and everyday deadly weapons – but the motto upon a portrait, said to be of Marlowe, at Corpus Christi College, Cambridge, says, *Quod me nutrit me destruit* ("That which nourishes me destroys me").[36] Marlowe mixed dark worlds and deep desires:

---

36 Although that motto, in another light, is simply a better educated version of the narrative of self-failure tattooed on the bodies of a majority of men in prisons: legends such as "Born to lose" and "Cut here".

> That like I best that flies beyond my reach.
> Set me to scale the high pyramids
> And thereon set the diadem of France;
> I'll either rend it with my nails to nought,
> Or mount the top with my aspiring wings,
> Although my downfall be the deepest hell.[37]

But though Marlowe's greatest creation, Dr Faustus, sold his soul to the devil for twenty-four years of wealth, power, and the uncovering of all the secrets of the world, Marlowe himself was no sorcerer but something much more dangerous. When a world collapses, everything may be called into question and, if the allegations laid against Marlowe by informers and by fellow playwright Thomas Kyd were true, Marlowe did indeed question everything: God, religion, sexuality, power. But, lest we forget the world of shattered mirrors that made men fools throughout these years, remember that Kyd spoke after torture, and Marlowe, a well-known friend and associate of Sir Walter Raleigh, may have been the victim of smears directed towards the downfall of his patron.

However, the mud stuck – and such mud. According to Kyd, "It was his custom ... to jest at the devine scriptures, gybe at praiers, & stryve in argument to frustrate & confute what hath byn spoke or wrytt by prophets & such holie men,"[38] and it is worth quoting in full the note delivered by professional informer Richard Baines to the Privy Council concerning Marlowe's views:

> That the Indians, and many authors of antiquity, have assuredly written of above 16 thousand years agone, whereas Adam is proved to have lived within six thousand years.

---

37 *The Massacre at Paris,* Marlowe, 1969, page 542.
38 "Introduction", in Marlowe, 1969, page 14.

He affirmeth that Moses was but a juggler, and that one Hariot being Sir Walter Raleigh's man can do more than he.

That Moses made the Jews to travel 40 years in the wilderness (which journey might have been done in less than one year) ere they came to the promised land, to the intent that those who were privy to many of his subtleties might perish, and so an everlasting superstition reign in the hearts of the people.

That the beginning of religion was only to keep men in awe.

That it was an easy matter for Moses being brought up in all the arts of the Egyptians to abuse the Jews, being a rude and gross people.

That Christ was a bastard and his mother dishonest.

That he was the son of a carpenter, and that if the Jews among whom he was born did crucify him, they best knew him and whence he came.

That Christ deserved better to die than Barabas, and that the Jews made a good choice, though Barabas were both a thief and a murderer.

That if there be any God or any good religion, then it is in the Papists, because the service of God is performed with more ceremonies, as elevation of the mass, organs, singing men, shaven crowns, etc. That all Protestants are hypocritical asses.

That if he were put to write a new religion, he would undertake both a more excellent and admirable method, and that all the New Testament is filthily written.

That the woman of Samaria and her sister were whores and that Christ knew them dishonestly.

That Saint John the Evangelist was bedfellow to Christ and leaned always in his bosom; that he used him as the sinners of Sodoma.

That all they that love not tobacco and boys are fools.

That all the apostles were fishermen and base fellows, neither of wit nor worth; that Paul only had wit, but he was a timorous fellow in bidding men to be subject to magistrates against his conscience.

That he had as good a right to coin as the Queen of England, and that he was acquainted with one Poole, a prisoner in Newgate, who hath great skill in mixture of metals, and having learned some things of him, he meant through help of a cunning stamp-maker to coin French crowns, pistolets, and English shillings.

That if Christ would have instituted the sacrament with more ceremonial reverence, it would have been in more admiration; that it would have been better much better being administered in a tobacco pipe.

That the angel Gabriel was bawd to the Holy Ghost, because he brought the salutation to Mary.

That one Richard Cholmley hath confessed that he was persuaded by Marlowe's reasons to become an atheist.[39]

Whether or not Marlowe really believed this is almost beside the point: that such ideas could be raised and seem credible shows how, in the shattering of the old medieval world view, everything had changed.

In such an atmosphere, where whispers and lies and innuendo could see even the most powerful men in the land brought down and which would have anyone without the highest patronage put

---

39   Source: http://www.wwnorton.com/college/english/nael/16century/topic_1/baines.htm.

to torture, it is no surprise that men sought power, and urgently. At a base level, it was a matter of self-preservation; at its highest, a manifesto of hope. Outside the nobility, there was a growing body of educated men who lacked the retainers, power, and influence of the old landed families, and were thus even more vulnerable to the vicissitudes of the time. In London, the lawyers of the Inns of Court formed an intellectual counterweight to the clergy, while the spread of printing and the increase in trade meant that the merchant and, increasingly, the artisan classes were becoming educated. Marlowe was the son of a shoemaker.

The two most important facts of London geography are the river and the people. The river divides and feeds the city, with food and money and ideas, while the people, the press and buzz and swirl of humanity, are the most important fact of the city. London exists because of, and for, and through, its very excess of people. Where the most important fact of existence becomes other people, and the powers they exercise over others, it becomes less extraordinary that a mind as caustic and creative as Marlowe's might have come up with such an extraordinary litany of abuse towards Christianity. For, looking around at the other world religions, it is clear that atheism is very much a product of Christianity, a consequence of aspects of Christian theology and Christian behaviour, rather than an independent critique of religion as such. No such streams of thought exist in the other great world religious cultures. How appropriate that the first great Christian atheist grew up amid the blood and paranoia of the Reformation: we should have known. All the reformers and the counter-reformers should have known: "Be not deceived; God is not mocked: for whatsoever a man soweth, that shall he also reap" (Galatians 6:7). We sowed blood and burning; we reaped defiance and despite.

But in his (alleged) atheism Marlowe was a man born out of time. The sixteenth century was not ready for such views and nor even was the seventeenth, despite the civil war that tore the country apart being in part the result of rival religious views. Even modern science, the fundamentally new way of viewing and manipulating the world that really got under way in the seventeenth century, owed much of its early appeal – indeed, its very legitimacy – to the religious convictions of its practitioners. Francis Bacon, the propagandist for the scientific method, saw this new way towards the Advancement of Learning as religiously sanctioned: "For as the Psalms and other scriptures do often invite us to consider and magnify the great and wonderful works of God, so if we should rest only in the contemplation of the exterior of them as they first offer themselves to our senses, we should do a like injury unto the majesty of God." God, a rational spirit, had made a rational creation, bound by laws which could be discovered, discerned, and understood.

Bacon was born on the Strand. Thomas Hobbes, on the other hand, was born in Wiltshire and spent much of his life travelling, but having written *Leviathan*, the book that was to make his name and remade political philosophy, he took refuge in London, on Fetter Lane. Published in 1651, *Leviathan* was written in the shadow of the English Civil War and the Thirty Years' War, the two conflicts that had devastated much of the continent in the first half of the century. In it, Hobbes sought to prove definitively that the secular authority was supreme. As England restored a monarchy and recovered from civil war, Hobbes' views began to seem a way through the contending views of the religious. But the man himself, despite the many accusations hurled against him, averred that he was a believer. "Do you think I can be an atheist and not know it?"[40] Besides, the Restoration in 1660 brought an end to religious enthusiasm: Charles II was no fanatic and his notoriously libertine

---

40 Quoted in Spencer, 2014, page 51.

court had little interest in theology when the days and nights could be spent in wit and sport, while the new mercantile spirit set about restoring the wealth of the nation.

Not everyone was pleased. John Milton, the great Puritan poet, wrote in 1673 that "it is a general complaint that this nation of late years is grown more numerously and excessively vicious than heretofore: Pride, Luxury, Drunkenness, Whoredom, Cursing, Swearing, bold and open atheism everywhere abounding".[41] But it was the genius of Charles II to fashion a century of religious toleration in England; even the deposition of his brother served to cement this general indifference to the different varieties of Christianity, as long as they were not tainted with the still unacceptable traces of Catholicism.

During the latter half of the seventeenth century and through the eighteenth century, what inclinations there were to atheism were subverted by the general atmosphere of religious laxity and the religiosity of the men involved in setting in motion the scientific revolution of the time. The Royal Society, founded in 1660 and given its royal charter in 1662, was the first organization devoted, as its full name states, to "the Improvement of Natural Knowledge"; that is, the scientific investigation of nature. Alongside theology and philosophy, there was a new pretender to the throne of truth, and one that, as its prestige grew, would come to supplant its elders in esteem. But among the early members of the Royal Society, and particularly those who were most important in the development of scientific knowledge, this was not seen to be the case. Robert Boyle, physicist and chemist and one of the key founding members of the Society, left money in his will for a series of annual lectures "for the defence of the Christian religion againt atheists and other unbelievers". These lectures continued until the mid-twentieth

---

41 Quoted in Spencer, 2014, page 73.

century and were revived in the twenty-first. After all, if the men actually uncovering nature's truth believed it to be simply another way of revealing God's glory, how could science be used against religion? If religion has its pantheon, so too does science, and sitting at the summit is the man who was also president of the Royal Society from 1703 to 1727: Isaac Newton.

It's pretty well impossible to overstate Newton's importance to the development of science, and his prestige matched his achievements. Alexander Pope, greatest of eighteenth-century poets, wrote in epitaph of the scientist:

> Nature and Nature's laws lay hid in night:
> God said, "Let Newton be!" and all was light.[42]

Newton split white light into colours, developed the reflecting telescope, invented calculus (although he spent many years involved in a bitter dispute with Gottfried Leibniz over priority), proposed the laws of motion and, most importantly of all in the minds of his contemporaries, discovered the law of gravity. By combining the laws of motion with the law of gravity, Newton was able to describe (and others, later, to predict) the motion of planets and stars, the movement of the tides, and the trajectories of ordinary bodies on earth (including falling apples!).

As the pre-eminent natural philosopher of his day, Newton's views mattered. The relative importance he placed on science and religion might be gauged by the fact that he spent as much of his adult life on biblical interpretation and understanding as he did upon science. Although Newton's views were unorthodox – he probably rejected belief in the Trinity – he did not make this aspect

---

42 Pope intended this epitaph for Newton's monument in Westminster Abbey, but the abbey authorities refused its addition, preferring instead a long-winded Latin inscription. Quoted in *Oxford Concise Dictionary of Quotations*, 2011, page 293.

of his faith public, while his religiosity *was* public, based on his writings, letters, and work. For example, in *The Mathematical Principles of Natural Philosophy*, Newton wrote:

> And from his true dominion it follows, that the true God is a Living, Intelligent and Powerful Being; and from his other perfections, that he is Supreme or most Perfect. He is Eternal and Infinite, Omnipotent and Omniscient; that is, his duration reaches from Eternity to Eternity; his presence from Infinity to Infinity; he governs all things, and knows all things that are or can be done. He is not Eternity or Infinity, but Eternal and Infinite; he is not Duration or Space, but he endures and is present.[43]

Thus the attitude of the standard-bearers of the new knowledge, coupled with the general distaste towards "enthusiasm" in religion that prevailed in England through most of the eighteenth century, made it difficult for those so inclined to kick against the pricks, since there was relatively little to goad them to anger. In contrast to other countries in Europe, Britain became known for its relative religious tolerance, and London in particular offered refuge to religious refugees from the continent.

There was one atheist comet in the late eighteenth to early nineteenth century, but Percy Bysshe Shelley was no Londoner, although he did take lodgings in the city at various times through his itinerant life. Shelley, though, was almost as much an outlier as Marlowe. Adolescent intellectual confidence allowed him to write, while at Oxford, *The Necessity of Atheism* and send it to the heads of the university's colleges (who, remember, were still required to be

---

43 "General Scholium" from *The Mathematical Principles of Natural Philosophy*, 1729. See: http://www.newtonproject.sussex.ac.uk/view/texts/normalized/NATP00056.

ordained in the Church of England and, generally, were expected to remain unmarried). He finished the pamphlet by concluding: "Every reflecting mind must allow that there is no proof of the existence of a Deity. Q.E.D." This suggests more the glibness of today's new unbelievers than the philosophical rigour of the great nineteenth-century atheists such as Feuerbach, Nietzsche, and Marx. This was atheism as adolescent rebellion, and the glamour that still attaches to the lives of Shelley and Byron (as opposed to their actual work) suggests that these most rock 'n' roll of poets still retain their paradoxical ability, considering they were both aristocratic to the core, to appear anti-establishment.

However, the mature Shelley was more pantheist than atheist. The first publicly avowed atheist in England, although remaining anonymous, outed himself in 1782, writing in an *Answer to Dr Priestley's Letters to a Philosophical Unbeliever*:

> As to the question whether there is such an existent Being as an atheist, to put that out of all manner of doubt, I do declare upon my honour that I am one. Be it therefore for the future remembered, that in London in the kingdom of England, in the year of our Lord one thousand seven hundred and 81, a man has publickly declared himself an atheist.[44]

The public atheist was probably a physician named Matthew Turner, and thus solidly a member of the middle classes. But the slowly building core of atheism in the later eighteenth and the nineteenth centuries had little to do with the upper or middle classes. It was rather a function of the huge disruptions and movements of the eighteenth and nineteenth centuries, as land was enclosed and a landless pool of labour created that found work in the newly industrializing towns of the north and, although this is

---

44   Quoted in Spencer, 2014, page 161.

seldom acknowledged, London too. Taken from the rhythms and conventions of rural life, and the pressure to conform exerted by gentry and neighbours, religious habits just... melted away.

In fact, if ever there was convincing proof of the idea that human beings are fallen creatures it lies in this: we shuck off good habits with barely a backwards glance – indeed, we feel a certain relief at their loss – but bad habits can hardly be shifted, despite employing all the strength and will available to us. The population movements of the eighteenth and nineteenth centuries confirm this: taken from their homes and communities, people abandoned their old ways and beliefs as easily as they shook the cowpats from their feet.

When, in the nineteenth century, reformers started to investigate the religious habits of poor Londoners, they were appalled. It wasn't really that the new working class disbelieved in God; rather that he, at least as he was presented to them by the church, appeared irrelevant. The City of London was well served – probably over-served – with churches, but the same was not true of London's ever-spreading suburbs. Between 1730 and 1815, when the city was growing fast, only ten or so new churches were built to serve the new urban areas. As early as 1786, reformers had noted "the great estrangement that has taken place between the lower orders of people and their parochial ministers".[45] But, in 1851, there came the evidence to back up the general suspicion that, somehow, faith had leaked away from the working classes inhabiting Britain's newly industrialized cities and, in particular, London.

The 1851 *Census of Religious Worship* investigated every place of worship in the country, including nonconformist chapels, synagogues, and Catholic churches. The survey was done alongside the national census that was being carried out at the same time,

---

45   Inwood, 1998, page 676.

and asked the respondents how many people (adults and children) attended church on Sunday, 30 March 1851. The churches were also asked whether this figure differed significantly from normal, when the church had been built, and how many people it could accommodate.

Once the numbers were crunched, it became clear that church attendance was poor in all Britain's cities, but worst of all in the working-class areas of London. At first glance, this might have been because there simply were not enough churches: there were 1,097 churches, chapels, and synagogues in London but, adding up their capacities, they could only hold 30 per cent of London's population. But despite this inadequate provision, London's churches were not full. On census Sunday, less than 20 per cent of Londoners went to a morning service and 13 per cent to an evening service (an unknown percentage attended both morning and evening, meaning that less than a third of Londoners attended church on Sunday). Churchgoing was more common in wealthier areas (39 per cent attending in Hampstead and 34 per cent in Wandsworth) and trailed away in the poorer parts of the city (15 per cent in the East End, 14 per cent in Bermondsey, and 9 per cent in Shoreditch).

Why didn't the poor go to church? This was the question the Victorians faced – and, as was the way with the Victorians, they tried their darnedest to answer the question too.

One obvious cause was the practice of pew renting. The Synod of Exeter in 1297 had declared the practice illegal, a judgement confirmed by the new secular authorities in 1612 that averred a church "is dedicated and consecrated to the service of God, and is common to all inhabitants", yet pew renting continued right up until 1970. A family could, with a discreet nod from churchwarden or vicar, rent a pew for their exclusive use; the ultimate expression of this was to be found in box pews, which were surrounded with wooden panelling and had gates and, sometimes, even fireplaces

– churches were often cold and draughty, and sitting through an hour-long sermon in the long, cold winters of the eighteenth and nineteenth centuries must have required considerable fortitude. These pews naturally came to be seen as family property, being passed down the generations and allowing all the members of a family to sit together at church. But, just as naturally, in a socially stratified society, they tended towards the marginalization and exclusion of the poor – quite literally, as those who did attend church had to sit on benches or stools, or stand, in the odd bits of space left over.

One frustrated churchgoer wrote in 1882: "I did go once, but the people were all shut in, and the folk in the boxes looked at me as if I had got in without paying: so after walking up and down several times, like a man in a station trying to get a seat when the train is full, I went home."[46]

Having identified a problem, the Victorians worked energetically to improve it, but the lack of accessible places to sit, and the sense of social inferiority that went with it, was not the only reason that the poor did not go to church. The reformers believed, probably rightly, that the working classes had not so much rejected Christianity but that there were few positive incentives to worship – and none of the social pressures that ensured the rural poor went, religiously, to church on Sunday.

One costermonger told the census: "Religion is a regular puzzle to the costers... the costers somehow mix up being religious with being respectable, and so they have a queer sort of feeling about it."[47] Many of the poor felt they were not wanted in church:

---

46 "Sacred Mysteries: Renting the Best Seats in the Church", by Christopher Howse, *The Telegraph*. http://www.telegraph.co.uk/news/religion/7693232/ Sacred-Mysteries-Renting-the-best-seats-in-church.html (accessed 9 July 2015).
47 Inwood, 1998, page 679.

I never goes to any church or chapel. Sometimes I hasn't clothes as is fit, and I s'pose I couldn't be admitted into sich fine places in my working dress. I was once in a church, but felt queer, as one does in them strange places, and never went again. They're fittest for rich people. Yes, I've heered about religion and God Almighty... I'm satisfied with what I knows and feels about it, and that's enough about it.[48]

This sort of exclusion did not end with the Victorians. I knew a builder, Arthur Dare, whose family were old East Enders but, like most East Enders when they'd made some money, he'd moved out, to Chingford. He did some work for my family and I enjoyed talking with him when he took his tea break, carefully rolling a cigarette and smoothing out his copy of the *Daily Mail* to read. When Arthur first began in the trade, he worked with men who had themselves started on sites at the beginning of the twentieth century, when it paid foremen to employ boys to go round the site searching for bent nails and straightening them. I don't think I've ever heard anything that so graphically illustrates the change in costs between labour and materials that has occurred over the last century. One afternoon, as we drank tea, Arthur told me how, as a young boy, he'd been quite religious until one day a parishioner, seeing him in his patched clothes, asked in the most supercilious of tones, "What are *you* doing here?" Arthur walked out of the church and never returned to it.

I wonder if that woman ever realized, before she died, what she had done.

Jesus said, "Let the little children come to me, and do not hinder them, for the kingdom of heaven belongs to such as these" (Matthew 19:14, NIV).

---

48 Inwood, 1998, page 680.

However, the avowed atheists of Britain's higher classes had little interest in the toilers. Shelley summed up their attitude: "Let this horrid Galilean rule the Canaille [the common people]. The reflecting part of the community, that part in whose happiness we have so strong an interest, certainly do not require his morality which when there is no vice fetters virtue."[49] Shelley also intimates another aspect of upper-class atheism: the freedom to indulge sexual appetites, freed from guilt, while making sure the lower classes aren't screwing around.

Chartism, the working-class movement for greater democracy and reform that flourished from 1838 to 1858, might have proved an avenue for radical atheism but many of its leaders, while not necessarily conventionally religious, often espoused Christian values. William Lovett, who founded the London Working Men's Association in 1836, said he was "of that religion which Christ taught, and which very few in authority practise".[50] Although Chartism ostensibly failed, it's worth noting that, of the six goals it sought by avowedly non-violent means, five have been implemented:

- votes for every man over twenty-one;

- secret ballots;

- no property qualification for MPs;

- MPs to be paid, so that a poor man might serve;

- and constituencies with equal numbers of voters.

Only the Chartists' sixth demand, of annual parliamentary elections, has not been enacted. We live now in a Chartist democracy, and

---

49 Jones, 1964, page 66.
50 Spencer, 2014, page 179.

the fact we do is due, in no small part, to the restraint of men like Lovett.

So while working-class anger was channelled into political action informed by Christian ideas of justice (it has often been remarked, with justification, that the Labour Party owed as much to Methodism as to Marx) the upper classes of Victorian England did what they always did when faced with a crisis: they formed clubs and societies.

Victorian Ethical Societies were the British version of Auguste Comte's religion of humanity, enabling like-minded people to gather together but without all that French flummery with ritual that put off Anglo-Saxons. For a visitor from another world, it might have been a little difficult to see how these meetings differed from low-church and chapel services:

> For the last four years I have been a member of one of the Ethical Societies and I can speak of the help and strength which it gives me in my duties to attend our Sunday meetings. Not only the addresses, but the instrumental music and singing, inspire me for the world of the coming week and rest me after that of the past. It is an unspeakable comfort to meet there others who are trying to surmount the difficulties of life in the ethical spirit.[51]

For some reformers, this church without God approach was too cooperative: religion was an enemy to be attacked, not something to be aped. Eleanor Marx, Karl Marx's daughter, said: "We think the Christian religion an immoral illusion, and we wish to use any argument to persuade the people that it is false. Ridicule appeals to the people we have to deal with, with much greater force than any amount of serious logical argument. We want to make

---

51   Spencer, 2014, page 189.

them disregard the mythical next world and live for this world."[52] Although Eleanor Marx proposed ridicule as a weapon, it was Charles Bradlaugh who perfected it.

Bradlaugh was born in 1833 in Hoxton and, apart from a couple of early years spent in Ireland as an enlisted soldier, he lived most of his life in the capital. In line with his medieval forebears, Bradlaugh was a lawyer, and a skilled one; to protect his employers from his growing notoriety he employed the highly suitable nom-de-plume of "Iconoclast". But his iconoclasm resulted from disillusion. Bradlaugh had been a religious boy, attending Sunday school and preparing for confirmation, until he asked some questions about the Church of England's Thirty-Nine Articles. In a classic example of how not to deal with an inquisitive sixteen-year-old, the vicar, rather than attempting to answer the questions or simply admitting he did not know, told Bradlaugh senior that his son was an atheist in the making and forbade his confirmation. Bradlaugh junior, who might otherwise have continued as the enthusiastic Sunday school teacher he was, left church and faith altogether, and employed his considerable rhetorical gifts to advance the cause of atheism and secularism, founding the National Secular Society in 1866 and remaining its president for the next quarter-century. As such, his combative style formed the secularist approach, ensuring that it became intertwined with atheism when, as the American model proves, the two are by no means necessary bedfellows.

Speaking of bedfellows, in 1877 Bradlaugh re-issued a notorious pamphlet on birth control with Annie Besant, fellow freethinker and the one-woman nexus where atheism and secularism met theosophism and clairvoyance. In a country where birth control was illegal (and fairly ineffective in any case), *The Fruits of Philosophy* (the rather unlikely title of the pamphlet) saw Bradlaugh and

---

52 Webb, 1979, page 302.

Besant charged with obscenity, and found guilty but acquitted on a technicality.

According to Bradlaugh – a man not given to shades of opinion – there were just two possible intellectual positions, only one of which was plausible:

> One, the completest submission of the intellect to authority: to some book, or church, or man. The other, the most thorough assertion of the right and duty of individual thought and judgement.[53]

No prizes for guessing which of the two Bradlaugh thought plausible. Still, it is good to see that the caricaturing of religious thought by the twenty-first century's new atheists has a solid historical foundation.

Bradlaugh's fame grew when he was elected to parliament in 1880 as MP for Northampton. As an atheist, he asked to be allowed to make an affirmation rather than swear the oath of allegiance. A parliamentary committee ruled against him and, since his seat thus became vacant, a new election was held in 1881 – and Bradlaugh won it. He won the elections in 1882, 1884, and 1885, and then held his seat in the general election of 1886 as well. The Speaker finally allowed Bradlaugh to take his seat after the final 1886 election and, in 1888, he succeeded in having a new Oaths Act passed through parliament, allowing the oath of allegiance to be affirmed rather than sworn before God.

With such a high-profile case, interest in atheism and secularism also increased, with membership of the National Secular Society reaching a peak at 4,000.

But then Bradlaugh was admitted to parliament, new MPs were allowed to affirm allegiance rather than swear to God, and all the

---

53   Marsh, 2011, page 83.

fuss vented slowly away before the British establishment's ability to give ground where necessary. Deprived of a reason for rage, Victorian atheism lost its verve and, when Bradlaugh died in 1891, the fire went out of the movement. It had won its motivating battle: there was an accepted place for an avowed atheist in the highest chamber of public debate in the land. Now, with that fight won, it was time to move wholeheartedly into the realm of ideas, and with a new generation of thinkers coming to the fore, it seemed that the dawn of the twentieth century would see the final end of religion in general and Christianity in particular as a credible intellectual movement.

From the Restoration up until the start of the twentieth century, the city's general attitude towards religion might be described, overall, as indifference. Oh, there was the Victorian revival, of course, when in reaction to the alarming evidence of the religious census of 1851, churches were built to serve the sprawling suburbs, and churchmen and women went on mission into darkest Hackney and foul St Giles. Yet the city remained steadfast in its orientation: God might be all very well, but money ruled the city. The expansion of trade that started during the reign of Charles II had grown explosively in the next 200 years, as London became both an industrial powerhouse in its own right – although its factories were smaller and less obvious than the great mills of the north – and, just as importantly, the main entry and exit port for trade with the rest of the world. Trade – free trade – became the city's god, for it brought incalculable wealth in its wake. The actual God stuff had to fit in around that and, in general, it did. The great intellectual assault on God in the nineteenth century was written largely in German: Nietzsche, Freud, Marx, Feuerbach, Strauss. Frankly, not much could have stood up to such an assault, and God wilted a bit under the pressure of all those really long words. The main British contribution was Darwin, and curiously, as he has come to play such an important role for twenty-first-century atheists, his was the least important contribution.

The heavy intellectual groundwork having been laid, English-speaking philosophers started poking at God's recumbent corpse, to make sure he stayed dead. Of these, the most high profile was Bertrand Russell. The Russells were an aristocratic family, his grandfather having been prime minister twice under Queen Victoria. Bertrand Russell's parents died when he was young and he was brought up by his grandmother – and various nannies and tutors – at Pembroke Lodge in Richmond Park. In his philosophy, Russell attempted to ground mathematics in logic, writing three volumes of *Principia Mathematica* to do so. This was a major element of the wider philosophical project to ground and verify language in logic; a project that became known as logical positivism.

The great proponent of this in Britain was the philosopher A. J. Ayer, a Londoner – but being a proper Londoner he was born of immigrant stock. He won a scholarship to Eton and became Grote Professor of the Philosophy of Mind and Logic at University College, London (which is where I went, eventually, to university, finally locating the library towards the end of my second year there). According to Ayer and the positivists, only scientific knowledge (that is, publically verifiable knowledge) is factual, and everything else – and Ayer particularly singled out the God language of theology – is literally meaningless. So rather than claiming that God does not exist, Ayer and the positivists argued that all the centuries of thought and speculation about him had been pointless, for such language contains no content: God was not so much dead as vacuous.

This was the fulfilment of one of the great attacks on belief. While it is, in principle, extremely difficult to prove a negative ("God does not exist"), what Ayer and co. had done was prove religious language meaningless: in talking of God, there was no there, there. Think of it like this. Suppose I were to say to you that last night I dreamed of you. Yes, you. Now, you don't know me and I don't know you, yet still I maintain I dreamed of you last night. You might believe me – I would imagine if you've read this far you might be inclined to follow me just that one little step further – but, on the other hand, maybe you do know me; then, like as not, you'd definitely not believe a word of it. In either case, though, my dream is not verifiable: I claim to have dreamed of you, but there is no way I can demonstrate this claim to anyone outside my own head.

God talk, according to Ayer, whether it be prayer or liturgy, the byways of systematic theology or the highways of Scripture, let alone the intensity of mystical experience, is like this: dream stuff locked into heads, having no more weight than words and considerably less substance.

There. That having been accomplished, humanity can get on with the serious business of sorting out the world.

And for a time in the mid-twentieth century it seemed as though this might happen. A. J. Ayer published *Language, Truth and Logic* in 1936 and it became an unlikely bestseller. "Freddie" Ayer, when he became a professor at UCL, took his place alongside Bertrand Russell as a major figure in London's social and literary scenes – at least, for that rarefied class of beings who live in the sort of circles where everyone they know lives in Zone 1. Their private lives were as turbulent as that of any of the movie stars of the era, with Russell marrying four times in between many affairs. Ayer also married four times – the third wife being the former spouse of Sir Nigel Lawson, which made him Nigella Lawson's stepfather – but he rather cheated by remarrying his first wife, so it was a case of four marriages and three wives. Both men were beloved of the camera and loved appearing on TV, they cultivated high profiles and were good value for them, and both attracted character anecdotes.

For instance, the nonagenarian Russell struck up an acquaintance with the young and beautiful actress Sarah Miles, who lived in the same Chelsea street as he did. Inviting her back to his house, he proceeded to demonstrate how to make the perfect cucumber sandwich – apparently the sliced cucumber should be so thin as to be translucent – while fondling Miles's thigh and peering down her blouse. Miles, a generous-minded young woman, allowed the old and lonely philosopher his fun.

Ayer, although not quite so old at seventy-seven, faced a more formidable foe: "Iron" Mike Tyson, heavyweight champion of the world and self-proclaimed baddest man on the planet. Ayer, always a social animal, had become friends with an American fashion designer, Fernando Sanchez. For the philosopher, this had the added bonus of bringing him into the orbits of beautiful young models when attending Sanchez's parties. Ayer was at one such party when an agitated woman rushed into the room, asking for help: her friend was being assaulted. Going to the woman's aid, Ayer found that the woman in question was a young and not-yet-famous Naomi Campbell, while the man pressing himself upon her was Mike Tyson. Ayer told Tyson to stop. Tyson, unused to anyone, let alone septuagenarians, telling him to stop doing anything, inquired if Ayer knew who he was: the heavyweight champion of the world. To which the unperturbed Ayer replied: "And I am the former Wykeham Professor of Logic. We are both preeminent in our field; I suggest that we talk about this like rational men."[54] Having seldom faced such front, Tyson started talking with Ayer, and Campbell made her getaway.

From this, it's easy to see why Ayer was such a superb subject for a biographer; how many other Wykeham Professors of Logic are samba dancers, or so cavalier towards lovers that they write

---

54   Rogers, 1999.

identical letters to two different mistresses, unaware that the women are friends? The women in question compared their notes!

Russell's tireless campaigning against nuclear weapons also raised his profile: his angular features and shock of white hair became the public face of philosophy in Britain. The two men might not have succeeded in killing off religion, but they had made the intellectual case for atheism; while it was obviously impossible to bury a non-existent being, at least his end was in sight. But God, whether or not he exists, is nothing if not slippery. Just when you think you've got him where you want him, he slips out of your grasp, and you find that all you're holding is yourself. So it turned out with logical positivism. Hang on a minute, said other philosophers, how do you verify the principle of verification? What experiment can you run on the scientific method itself?

Turns out, logical positivism was self-contradictory and, what was worse, one of the great lines of attack on God – that all God talk was nonsense – had in fact succeeded only in digging up the ground on which atheists found certainty: logic and mathematics. Ayer fought the good fight gamely, but towards the end of his life even he realized the game was up. When he was interviewed and asked about the flaws in logical positivism, he replied with disarming honesty: "Well, I suppose the most important defect was that nearly all of it was false."[55]

Towards the end of his life, Ayer died – and then came back to life again. His near-death experience included an awareness of a (rather painful) red light that governed the universe and its two slightly incompetent ministers in charge of space, who had failed in their last inspection and left space out of joint. Ayer, being Ayer even though dead, decided to put them right, but unfortunately his experience ended before he could tell God how to run things better.

---

55   Magee, 1978, page 131.

It made little difference to his fundamental beliefs: "So there it is. My recent experiences have slightly weakened my conviction that my genuine death, which is due fairly soon, will be the end of me, though I continue to hope that it will be. They have not weakened my conviction that there is no god."[56]

For myself, I profess admiration for an atheist who sticks to his unbelief with all the stubborn self-regard of the band of defiant dwarves in *The Last Battle*. "The dwarfs are for the dwarfs," as they said, while sticking fingers in their ears and screwing up their eyes, and I suspect that God will greet with more respect the atheist who looks him in the face and still proclaims his defiance than the one who cowers. For one thing writing this chapter has taught me is that the root of atheism is not disbelief in God's existence but rather savage fury at the world and people God has made; the only way to get him back is to refuse him.

This savage fury is the defining characteristic of the New Atheism. Rather than fading gently from public life, God and his believers were back – sometimes in the most savage and bloodstained of forms. The old secure belief that religion would fade away as modernization spread around the world proved false.

On 18 September 2010 an old man knelt in silent prayer before the Eucharist. There was nothing particularly unusual about that. What was unusual was that he was praying in company with 80,000 other people in Hyde Park. The old man was Pope Benedict XVI and I was one of the people kneeling on the grass in the twilight. The sounds of London receded. Around me in the crowd I saw grand old English ladies in tweed and pearls, Nigerians in traditional dress, Filipinos, South Americans, Poles and Italians, Indians and Sri Lankans (Tamil and Sinhala – and yes, they do look different if you know what to look for). All the peoples of the world, who meet

---

56 *Sunday Telegraph*, 28 August 1988. Reproduced online: http://www. philosopher.eu/others-writings/a-j-ayer-what-i-saw-when-i-was-dead/.

and live in the city, were there, praying in silence before the Lord in the company of the pope.

And earlier that day I'd been to see the protest march against Pope Benedict's visit and, you know, I don't think I've ever seen a whiter, more middle-class group of people in London. And the self-righteous sanctimoniousness dripping from face and placard and Stephen Fry made even the most unctuous of believers seem a model of self-reflection by comparison.

As we travelled home in the tube that night, and saw other families waving their yellow papal flags not in triumph but in sheer joy, I knew I'd made the better choice.

CHAPTER 6

THIS CHARMING MAGIC

"The ultimate book for those who would walk with the Gods." That was the sell line that made me pick up the big, thick, green book from a shelf in Watkins. I was in my late teens and I wanted... I wanted to mean something and to understand more, to escape myself and to be myself; I wanted renown and adventure and to tear the veil of the living and to see the secrets of the dead and I wanted love and respect and clear skin and a girl to fall in love with; I wanted to be set free of me. I wanted power. Power to make all this happen, power not to be a tongue-tied schoolboy riding the 29 bus down Green Lanes into town, with my birthday money tight-fisted in my pocket, to seek knowledge in the pages of my truest loves and in their sanctifying halls.

The bookshops of Tottenham Court Road and Cecil Court were my first solo destination; I'd catch the 29 bus early on Saturday morning after it turned out of Wood Green bus garage, climb to the top deck, and hide behind my book as the bus rolled slowly south, picking out my journey in chapters, safe from intrusion behind my walls of story.

Those were the days when Foyles was an outpost of Stalinist Russia, although with more stock. It seemed as if every book ever printed was there, somewhere, stacked ceiling-high under the fading names of each publisher. I still remember the battered desks where your books were wrapped with paper and you were given "the chit" to be presented to the enclosed, armoured cubicle where the treasurer sat clinking behind towers of change, to pay and then return, chit stamped, to claim the books as, now, your own.

But even Foyles did not have "The ultimate book for those who would walk with the Gods". That was in Watkins, together with strange smells and stranger people, whose scrutinizing glances I ignored – if there was one lesson I had learned early as a child of the city, it was to make eye contact with no one.

It was about the thickest book I'd ever seen – 800 pages – and above the solid black of the sell line the title, just two words: *The Occult*.

London is a magical city. Oh, yes, the countryside is the haunt of wise women, the cunning folk of craft and herb and old lore, but the city is the place for sorcerers, for the seekers after arcane knowledge and the power it promises.

Contrary to popular belief, witch hunts were not features of medieval society. It was only in the sixteenth century that they became widespread, as people sought explanation and scapegoats for the ills of the century. The king himself, while reigning as James VI in Scotland, wrote a treatise against witchcraft:

The fearefull aboundinge at this time in this countrie, of these detestable slaues of the Deuill, the Witches or enchaunters, hath moved me (beloued reader) to dispatch in post, this following treatise of mine, not in any wise (as I protest) to serue for a shew of my learning & ingine, but onely (mooued of conscience) to preasse thereby, so farre as I can, to resolue the doubting harts of many; both that such assaultes of Sathan are most certainly practiced, & that the instrumentes thereof, merits most severly to be punished.[57]

The witch persecutions of the late sixteenth and early seventeenth centuries were mainly directed at the poor and the old, lonely women living on the edges of villages made suspicious and paranoid by the traumas of the time. As the old institutions, in particular monasteries, charged with caring for the poor and elderly were dissolved, the support of them came on to communities, themselves hard-pressed amid poor harvests and bouts of disease. If there was a pattern, it was this: an old woman seeks aid of a neighbour but is refused. When the old woman persists, she is insulted and teased and, in the only form of retaliation available to her, she curses the uncharity of her neighbour. But then, should misfortune strike in the days or weeks immediately afterwards, it was no hard leap from the evil of the day to the harsh words of the old beggar woman.

The records show that the witch craze was worst in Essex. This may be an artefact of the haphazard nature of record-keeping – it's hard to see why this county should be worse than any other – but whether true or not, in the city there were others, much more highly connected, who sought knowledge and power through the occult arts.

The world had split in the sixteenth century. Religion was broken from its former unity. News of new worlds beneath the moon, lands unknown to the ancients, opened possibilities undreamed of and brought rumour of wealth unbounded. The heavens themselves shifted, and all that had been secure seemed unfixed and drifting.

In medieval story there is, in one sense, plenty of "magic". Merlin does this or that "by his subtilty", Bercilak resumes his

---

57 Source: http://www.gutenberg.org/files/25929/25929-h/25929-h.html.

severed head. But all these passages have unmistakably the note of "faerie" about them.... But in Spenser, Marlowe, Chapman, and Shakespeare the subject is treated quite differently. "He to his studie goes"; books are opened, terrible words pronounced, souls imperiled. The medieval author seems to write for a public to whom magic, like knight-errantry, is part of the furniture of romance: the Elizabethan, for a public who feel that it might be going on in the next street...[58]

The magic of London was not the hedge craft of country wise women but a high magic, an integral part of the Renaissance programme to reclaim the lost knowledge of the ancients. The sorcerers of the city were not the poor and the old and the female, but men of wealth who sought power – and they needed money in order to find and buy the grimoires and telescopes and alembics and athanors needed to practise the craft.

The astrologers who had so signally failed in their predictions that Anne Boleyn would bear a son had been banished from Henry's court, but by the time Elizabeth came to power, the melding of philosophy, occult knowledge, and early scientific speculations was well advanced. No one typified this better than John Dee. Mathematician, astrologer, alchemist, and magician, Dee was born in London but, as is the way with most of us born in the city, his parents weren't: they were Welsh. Adopted into the patronage system for his learning, he was asked to calculate the most propitious date and time for Elizabeth's coronation. Now a royal favourite, Dee travelled through Europe collecting books and knowledge. On his return, Dee set up his first alchemical laboratory and began his angelic conversations with the aid of a medium, Edward Kelley. Dee and Kelley travelled through Europe with their families, eventually fetching up in Bohemia, where

---

58 Lewis, 1973, pages 11–12.

Kelley's angel contact informed the men that they should hold all things in common, including their wives. "It was agreed by us to move the question, whether the sense were of Carnal use (contrary to the law of the Commandment) or of Spiritual love."[59] As Dee was sixty and Kelley thirty-two at the time, this command probably held more interest for Kelley than for Dee. Whether or not they did share wives is unclear, but the circumstantial evidence is suggestive: shortly after the command, Dee broke off his partnership with Kelley and returned to England, where his wife gave birth to a baby boy some nine months after the breaking of their fellowship. Whatever Dee's doubts, he raised the boy as his own.

Looking backwards from our twenty-first-century vantage point, we naturally elide sorcerers and astrologers, but from the perspective of the time, these were callings that presupposed very different views of the human place in the world. For the astrologer, man lived under the domination of the stars, his life and destiny laid out by the movement of the heavenly spheres. But the Renaissance sorcerer, the man of high magic, saw human beings as the measure of all things, and able to become anything, from angel to demon. The melding of neo-Platonism with various gnomic texts from antiquity, such as Pythagoras, Apuleius, and the Orphic and Sibylline books by the Florentines Marsilio Ficino and Pico della Mirandola, had produced a universe teeming with spirits intermediate between the human and angelic levels: daemons (not demons), aerii homines, genii. These were beings of power, which the man of wisdom might summon and control, thus gaining mastery.

The sixteenth century was when key thinkers began to suspect that it might be possible for mankind to seize control of his destiny, to break the power of the stars and wrest control of the earth from the elements. But how to do it? Magic was one, but another method

---

59   Source: http://www.oxforddnb.com/view/article/7418?docPos=1.

presented itself: science. Although now we see these as opposed, then there was little to choose between them: both presented themselves as manifestos of human emancipation.

Magic is power. Science is power. As the centre of political and mercantile power, London attracted and produced men committed to the new learning. One of the key players was born in York House on the Strand in 1561. Back then, the mansions of the elite lined the river that ran behind the Strand, as boats provided a much more reliable means of transport than anything on dry land. Although York House and the other mansions on the Strand were sold off to developers in the seventeenth century, in one of those strange survivals of previous ages that pop up in the city, the house's water gate remains, stranded and gently eroding in Victoria Embankment Gardens at the end of Buckingham Gardens. As this was where ships used to moor, its present distance from the river is a signal reminder of just how narrow a channel the Thames now occupies compared to its previous tidal spread.

It was Francis Bacon, the father of scientific empiricism, who was born in York House. In 1620 he published the *Novum Organum* (New Method) of knowledge, advancing the idea that by inductive reasoning and the interrogation of nature man might advance to greater knowledge of, and power over, nature.

The key question for the men of the time was which method would prove more fruitful. Science proceeds by virtue of its method, which means that while it might take a genius such as Newton or Einstein to propose a new theory, once published it is possible for anyone of reasonable intelligence to follow the reasoning by which they came to their conclusions. Similarly, science is demonstrated by experimenters of genius, like Michelson and Morley, running tests to show if predictions match results. But, once the experiment has first been run, anyone following the same method should be able to replicate the results.

Science is repeatable. That's its point. It might take a genius to find the path through the overwhelming array of data, but once the path is found any Tom, Dick, or Harry should be able to follow it.

The point of magic is that any Tom, Dick, or Harry *cannot* do it. A magician, a wizard might take years to learn a spell, a craft, a potion, but even if I followed the same practices as diligently and for as long, there would be no guarantee that I could repeat the spell. Magic is personal and particular. In that it resembles elite sport or virtuoso musicians. I might practise batting for as long as Kevin Pietersen, working as diligently as he does, and yet at the end of it I would not be able to do what he does. Why not? The short answer: I don't have his talent. The slightly longer answer: I do not have the combination of physical, mental, and emotional characteristics that make him a great batsman – my deficiencies ranging from poorer eyesight and being a good six inches shorter through to lacking a taste for physical confrontation as confirmation of my own abilities.

Similarly with music. *Pace* Malcolm Gladwell, but while 10,000 hours of practice might be necessary for mastery of an art, it is not necessarily sufficient for it. I could have set aside eight hours every day on the guitar – I did, for a number of years – and yet I never even came close to mastering the instrument, and this for a particular combination of physical and psychological reasons. To coin Albert's law: practice is necessary for mastery of an art but it is not sufficient for it; you need talent too. And by talent I mean the particular combination of physical, psychological, and spiritual traits that are necessary for a particular person to master a particular skill – and note that these will differ according to both the person and the art.

Similarly with magic. A wizard is, by nature, singular. Magic is performance and few have the talent for it.

So, in the theatre of public results, science won hands down in the seventeenth and eighteenth centuries: gravitation and the laws of motion, electricity and inoculation – all of these and more served to raise the prestige of science, as did the foundation of the Royal Society. The old ways and beliefs were passing, and the world had lost some of its enchantment, as evinced in Bishop Corbet's "Farewell to the Fairies":

> Witness those rings and roundelays
> Of theirs, which yet remain,
> Were footed in Queen Mary's days
> On many a grassy plain;
> But since of late, Elizabeth,
> And later, James came in,
> They never danced on any heath
> As when the time hath been.
>
> By which we note the Fairies
> Were of the old Profession,
> Their songs were "Ave Mary's",
> Their dances were Procession.
> But now, alas, they all are dead,
> Or gone beyond the seas;
> Or farther for Religion fled,
> Or else they take their ease.[60]

But unlike the fairies, magic did not go away.

London is a magical city. London is a mysterious city. And its magic and its mystery can come upon you at the most unexpected time. A small tree, seen by the path's edge on your daily walk and barely noticed so that its absence is not registered, nor its presence, until one day, in physical memory, I look and see that sometimes it is there and sometimes not.

---

60 Source: http://www.bartleby.com/40/179.html.

London is not like Venice, whose mystery is entwined in its labyrinth of streets and alleys, and in its beauty. For sure, London has its courtyards and dead ends, but a proper Londoner knows his patch. No, the mystery of London is in its familiar places, when the life drops away from them and the noise of the city dies down, and walking down a suburban street as twilight draws in I realize that all it would take is a slight twist of the real and I could keep walking down this street forever. But then, I live in the modern world, where the veil between worlds has been worn thin and we are kept from such sights only by a furious effort of will and a tumult of distraction. The walls were thicker two centuries ago, at the start of the Victorian age. Now, in retrospect, it takes on the antiquated air of its sepia-stained photographs, but it was the first, and perhaps only, truly modern age. It plucked the fruits of the Age of Enlightenment in the extraordinary range and power of its invention, which saw iron tracks grid the country and, in the city, the feats of tunnelling that produced the Underground and, even more importantly, the great sewerage system of Joseph Bazalgette, which made the megacity that London was becoming habitable.

The nineteenth century was the Age of Science undefiled. It was a time before the carnage of industrial war and the obscenity of research turned to death sullied the purity of the endeavour. This was the high point of reason and the lowest tide of superstition, when it seemed that everything would be illuminated and made clear. In comparison, our own age, with its proliferating cults and therapies, is a sink of superstition.

And yet... This time of reason was when many of the most important occult societies and organizations were formed, a shadow drop to the bright light of the age, and London, the city of cities throughout the Victorian age, was where many of the most important and enduring started or flourished: the Hermetic Order of the Golden Dawn, spiritualism, the Theosophical Society, the Ancient Order of Druids. (The Ancient Order of Druids is the oldest, having been founded in 1781 in the King's Arms pub, Poland Street, just off Oxford Street. There's a plaque outside the pub commemorating the fact. The pub itself is now a favourite with London's bears and otters. If you don't know what that means, it would probably be better to pick somewhere else for a swift half.)

Spiritualism, the contacting of the dead through mediums, first began in New York in 1848 but spread rapidly through America and Britain. It was unusual among the new religious movements of the time in being largely led by women, most of whom were working class. The most famous proponent of spiritualism was a man whose literary creation incarnated objective rationality at its most cerebral: Arthur Conan Doyle's Sherlock Holmes is a definitive London character, but the writer's own time living in the city was relatively brief. The Doyle family moved to London in 1891 when Arthur set up a medical practice at 2 Upper Wimpole Street, but they only lived in the city for two years; the diagnosis of Conan Doyle's wife, Louise, with tuberculosis demanded a move to somewhere with cleaner air. Conan Doyle, a doctor, lived with death; Louise died in 1906, and his eldest son, Kingsley, died in 1918 from complications of the wounds he suffered during the Battle of the Somme. Although raised a Catholic, Conan Doyle had lost his faith in his teens, but he acquired a keen interest in psychic research, joining the society dedicated to that in 1887. In 1916, Conan Doyle declared his belief in spiritualism, and as further family members died his faith strengthened. The believer did not influence the writer, however: Sherlock Holmes remained the sceptic through to his final written adventure, *The Adventure of Shoscombe Old Place*.

Spiritualism itself reached a plateau in the late nineteenth and early twentieth centuries, then fell away to some extent under the assault of debunkers and the vapidity of conversations with the dead: truly, if death was like this, an eternal Sunday in an out-of-season English seaside resort might be better. But conversations with the dead continue today throughout London; spiritualists are condescended to by sceptics and religious believers alike, metropolitans seeing them as polyester-clad suburbanites who are terminally uncool, while the official churches look and recoil at what this mirror of belief reveals. Are they all, our creeds and temples and liturgies, simply a recoil from the face of death?

The Theosophical Society also had its origin in New York – perhaps indicating how the centre of modernity was moving westward. The two key figures in its early development were both women: Helena Petrovna Blavatsky and Annie Besant, whom we have already met. Blavatsky (1831–91) was a Russian/German who had travelled widely in her youth and was the very antithesis of the Victorian ideal of womanhood. Alfred Sinnett, editor of *The Pioneer* newspaper on which Rudyard Kipling put in his "seven years' hard", described her thus:

> She was rugged and eccentric in appearance; she dressed
> anyhow – in loose wrappers – and smoked cigarettes
> incessantly. Worse than this, she was passionate and
> excitable, and often violent in her language. Namby-pamby
> conventionality shrank from her aghast – to her grim
> satisfaction, for she loathed it. She had a loud voice, that grew
> harsh in its tones when she felt irritated, and something or
> other would irritate her fifty times a day.[61]

When Blavatsky arrived in America, she became involved with the burgeoning spiritualist movement as a medium, but differed from its mainstream in maintaining that the communications she received

---

61 *Review of Reviews*, 3, 551, quoted in *Oxford Dictionary of National Biography*, http://www.oxforddnb.com/view/article/40930.

were not from the dead but other spirits. Blavatsky also claimed that during her travels she had met and studied with many religious teachers, even entering Tibet – which was closed to Westerners in the nineteenth century – and receiving a commission from the Masters of the Ancient Wisdom, a group of spiritual masters, to advance theosophy, the wisdom underlying all the world religions. To that end, Blavatsky founded the Theosophical Society in New York in 1875. An indefatigable traveller, Blavatsky moved to India and also visited Sri Lanka (then Ceylon), before returning to Europe and settling in London, where she met and became friends with Annie Besant. In the capital, Blavatsky founded an eponymous lodge, of which she was most definitely queen bee. W. B. Yeats, whom we shall meet again, joined the lodge and gives, in one of his letters, a masterly little portrait of the atmosphere after Blavatsky had expelled three members:

> Madame Blavatsky is in high spirits. The society is like the "happy family" that used to be exhibited round Charing Cross station – a cat in a cage full of canaries. The Russian cat is beginning to purr now and smoothen its furr again – The canary birds are less by three – The faithful will be more obedient than ever.[62]

Despite her professed universalism, Blavatsky saw the religions of the East – in particular Hinduism and Buddhism – as the greater vehicles for the spiritual advance of humanity. In her book *Isis Unveiled*, which lays out the doctrine of the great souled ones – the mahatmas – whom she claimed to be in contact with, Blavatsky attacks, with all the considerable vigour she could summon, what might be called the materialist trinity she held most responsible for the spiritual desiccation of Western civilization: David Hume,

---

62 *Collected Letters of W. B. Yeats*, vol. 1, page 162.

T. H. Huxley, and Charles Darwin. Indeed, such was her dislike of Darwin that she kept a stuffed baboon in her room, complete with spectacles, wing collar, morning coat, and tie, and with *The Origin of Species* under its arm.

It was, perhaps, no surprise that the mercantile and then imperial adventure that had taken Englishmen and women to the ends of the earth might, in the end, return and, returning, claim that what it had found was greater than what it had brought. The Theosophical Society is a key marker in the transformation of Western ideas relating to the East, although whether the change from material condescension to spiritual fascination was actually an advance, I am not at all sure.

Blavatsky's two-volume *magnum opus*, *The Secret Doctrine*, subtitled "The Synthesis of Science, Religion and Philosophy", which pretty well sums up its ambition, was published in 1888. Among the reviewers was the radical freethinker Annie Besant. For Besant, "Ever more and more had been growing on me the feeling that something more than I had was needed for the cure of social ills.... since 1886 there had been slowly growing up a conviction that my philosophy was not sufficient; that life and mind were other than, more than, I had dreamed."[63] Then she was asked to review *The Secret Doctrine*. The book came as revelation. "I was dazzled, blinded by the light in which disjointed facts were seen as parts of a mighty whole, and all my puzzles, riddles, problems, seemed to disappear.... in that flash of illumination I knew that the weary search was over and the very Truth was found."[64]

Besant asked to meet Blavatsky and, after only the shortest of hesitations, joined the Theosophical Society, even though this meant a break with all that she had already done and achieved in her life:

---

63 Besant, 2004.
64 Besant, 2004.

Was I to plunge into a new vortex of strife, and make myself
a mark for ridicule – worse than hatred – and fight again
the weary fight for an unpopular truth? Must I turn against
Materialism, and face the shame of publicly confessing that I
had been wrong, misled by intellect to ignore the Soul? Must
I leave the army that had battled for me so bravely, the friends
who through all brutality of social ostracism had held me dear
and true?[65]

But Besant had never lacked courage. She turned her back on her
old life, and invited Blavatsky to live at her house at 19 Avenue
Road, St John's Wood (walking past this house today, it would
appear that Besant's fight for socialism had not adversely affected
her own financial status). For her part, Blavatsky saw in Besant a
woman after her own mind and heart, and appointed her "in the
name of the Master [...] Chief Secretary of the Inner Group of
the Esoteric Section & Recorder of the Teachings"[66] so that, when
Blavatsky died on 8 May 1891, Besant took over as the leader of the
Theosophical Society.

Among the many visitors to Blavatsky in London was a
young Indian lawyer, Mohandas Gandhi. So she really did meet
a mahatma. And Besant moved to India in 1893, remaining there
for the rest of her life, joining the Indian National Congress in
1913 and becoming one of the fiercest opponents of the British
Raj – while Mahatma Gandhi was content to call a truce with the
Raj during World War I, Besant did no such thing, leading to her
internment. Such a fiery woman found Gandhi's method of non-
violent resistance unpalatable and she lost influence in Congress,
but remained president of the Theosophical Society until her

---

65   Besant, 2004.
66   Blavatsky, nd, vol. XII, page 485. http://www.katinkahesselink.net/
blavatsky/articles/v12/y1890_052.htm.

retirement. Besant died on 20 September 1933 in Adyar, now a suburb of Chennai, and was cremated on the shore.

And all I can say is that there's no one more intrepid than an intrepid Victorian woman.

As for the Hermetic Order of the Golden Dawn, this short-lived occult group was possibly the most influential of all the magical orders of Victorian England. It was founded in 1888 by William Woodman, William Westcott, and Samuel MacGregor Mathers, its doctrines and practices a melange of Hermeticism, kabbalah, mysticism, theosophy, and ritual magic. Its first temple was in London, at 19 Fitzroy Street (now a rather undistinguished office block fittingly unmarked by any blue plaque), and it soon attracted many celebrity Victorian adherents – this all being done by word of mouth and introduction, as the order remained secret at this time. Among its adepts were W. B. Yeats (of course – there scarcely seemed to be an esoteric order which he did not join), Irish revolutionary (and Yeats's muse) Maud Gonne, writer Arthur Machen, theatre producer and heiress Annie Horniman, and the actress and feminist Florence Farr. I have a particular soft spot for Farr as, in later life, she sold up all her possessions and moved to Sri Lanka (then Ceylon) to become principal at a newly established school for girls in Jaffna. There she learned to speak and read Tamil, sending Yeats her translations of Tamil poetry. Farr died in 1917; her body was burned according to Hindu custom and her ashes scattered in the Kelani River.

But the most significant new member of the order, at least as far as the Golden Dawn itself was concerned, was Aleister Crowley, the most notorious occultist of the twentieth century. Crowley was introduced into the order by Allan Bennett (not to be confused with Alan Bennett, bespectacled playwright). Bennett went on to become a Buddhist in Ceylon and then an ordained monk, before returning to London and introducing Buddhism to the West.

Crowley soon became dissatisfied with the level of knowledge to which he had access – patience does not seem to have been his most notable characteristic – and, going over the heads of the other Golden Dawn members in London, appealed to Mathers, who was then living in Paris. Mathers imposed Crowley upon the London group, leading to a full schism: the Hermetic Order of the Golden Dawn became, in short order – deep breath – Alpha and Omega (led by Mathers); Stella Matutina (which Yeats joined); the Holy Order of the Golden Dawn (of which more anon); and Astrum Argentum (Crowley's version of the order which, coming nicely up to date, is now on Facebook). Not so surprising when you think of the collection of talents and egos that went into creating the Golden Dawn in the first place.

As these successor orders each went their own way, they attracted new adherents. Few were of the calibre of the original members, with one exception: in 1917, Charles Williams was initiated into the Holy Order of the Golden Dawn.

Who was Charles Williams? If you haven't heard of him, you will know two of the men with whom he was, later, to be most closely associated: C. S. Lewis and J. R. R. Tolkien. Williams was born in 1886 and lived as a child – I'm delighted to say – in Holloway, walking the same streets I walked as a boy. His family was poor and, though he won an Intermediate Scholarship to University College, London, he only attended for two years before poverty forced him to leave without completing his degree. After working as a clerk for four years, he found a job as a proofreader at the London offices of the Oxford University Press. He remained with the OUP until he died. It transformed him, but he profoundly affected it too, writing a play, performed by his co-workers at the Press, that turned the daily round of publishing – editing, proofreading, and the apparently petty relationships of office life – into poetry and ritual. *The Masque of the Manuscript* delighted his colleagues, as did the man himself.

"He found the gold in all of us and made it shine.... By sheer force of love and enthusiasm he created about him an atmosphere that must be unique in the history of business houses."[67]

Such was Williams' public face. By all accounts he was a man of whom opinions were transformed through personal intercourse:

> he was tall, slim, and straight as a boy, though grey-haired. His face we thought ugly: I am not sure that the word "monkey" has not been murmured in this context. But the moment he spoke it became, as was also said, like the face of an angel – not a feminine angel in the debased tradition of some religious art, but a masculine angel, a spirit burning with intelligence and charity.[68]

The peculiar transformation he had effected on the atmosphere at Oxford University Press was, in part, a result of his particular manners – manners that "implied a complete *offer* of intimacy without the slightest *imposition* of intimacy".[69] But if that seems like a man too good to be true, there was another side of Williams – one apparent to anyone who has read the "supernatural shockers", the seven novels for which he is best known. For those who have not read them – and I suggest you do, but not until you've finished reading this book – a taste of their unique atmosphere is conveyed by the opening of *War in Heaven*: "The telephone bell was ringing wildly, but without result, since there was no-one in the room but the corpse",[70] or *All Hallows' Eve*, where a woman waiting on Westminster Bridge for her husband realizes that she is, in fact,

---

67 Carpenter, 1997, page 87.
68 Lewis, 1966, page ix.
69 Lewis, 1966, pages ix–x.
70 Williams, 1994.

dead. Present through all of the books is a taste for and an abiding interest in the occult. Of course – for Williams was a magician.

Now the Holy Order of the Golden Dawn, as reconstituted after the great schism, was more interested in mysticism than magic, and more Christian than pagan, but Williams, judging by his novels, certainly had a greater than working knowledge of "Goetia" – black magic. He once confided to a friend that "[a]t bottom a darkness has always haunted me"[71] and this darkness found expression, in words, through the mages and demons of his novels and, in his life, through an unusual capacity to understand evil. Williams' father had taught him how to assume, for argument's sake, views opposed to his own and that, coupled with his own dabblings, allowed him imaginative entry into a world where Platonic archetypes stalk English country lanes and sorcerers raise the dead that they might live forever.

For Williams, a lifelong Londoner, the city was the City – where temporal and eternal met and mixed, where the spirits of the dead mingled with the living, and the paving stones on which he trod were the paths of the City of God – and of the damned. There could be no clearer vision of the inhering of the supernatural in the natural, of the magical in the everyday. This vision that Williams offers, with free and open hand to anyone who reads his work, is his particular gift to those who now walk through the West End and in the dark shadow of the towers of the City.

So what of *The Occult*, "the ultimate book for those who would walk with the Gods"? Its author, Colin Wilson, exemplified the trajectory of post-war thought as well as anyone – as well as being an object lesson in the growing dangers of fame. Born in 1931, Wilson came from a working-class family and was self-taught. Originally from Leicester, he moved to London and, famously, dossed in a

---

71   Carpenter, 1997, page 80.

sleeping bag on Hampstead Heath at night while researching and writing his first book, *The Outsider*, in the Reading Room of the British Library. *The Outsider*, a study and invention of the outsider figure through the literature and arts of the nineteenth and early twentieth centuries, was a tremendously exciting book, made more so by the fact that its author, who seemed to me to have read absolutely everything, was only twenty-four when it came out. The book was a huge hit and Wilson suddenly found himself catapulted from a park bench in Hampstead to the height of literary – and tabloid – celebrity; a fame he took to with all the self-assurance of a man who had confided to his diary that he was "the major literary genius of our century". Unfortunately, the diary was published, in the *Daily Mail*, along with news of the enraged father of his girlfriend, armed with a horsewhip, breaking into a dinner party and accusing him of being "a homosexual with six mistresses" before setting about him with the whip.[72] Wilson took refuge in Cornwall, married the girlfriend, and set about writing books on the occult and crime while the literary establishment, without even the grace of a blush of embarrassment, set about trashing the reputation of a man they had, a few months earlier, hailed at his own estimation.

So the city, within its strict circles of power, excludes and exiles, that the powerful remain in power. However, Wilson was as much saved by his vanity as condemned by it. Ignored and ridiculed by the literary establishment, he wrote continuously, finding new readers among the young and the curious – myself not least among them. At least in my generation, it seems as if almost everyone, growing up, had a Colin Wilson moment, when one or another of his books opened our eyes to some new facet of experience or reality that the wider world ignored, and for me it was the paranormal, the strange, *The Occult*. Reading the book and its litany of wonders and oddities,

---

72 *The Guardian* obituary: http://www.theguardian.com/books/2013/dec/09/colin-wilson.

Wilson woke me from my dogmatic slumber, the belief, nurtured by my holy books – *The Dragons of Eden, The Ascent of Man* among others – that science, the study of the material world, might explain everything about the world. Turned out the world was strange: I had a book to prove it and, now, a reason to embrace the worlds of my childhood reading: worlds of wonder.

So I started exploring the occult: numerology, meditation, chiromancy, tarot, astrology, magic. I tried them all in the flush and fire of enthusiasm that can only be summoned by a mind fresh and unburdened with any great weight of knowledge, and with all the untrammelled egotism of a teenager: here was actual reason to think about... me! In numerology, the version of my name I preferred – Eddie Albert – made me, unfortunately, a 4: "the number of failure, poverty and general gloom",[73] whereas my birth name, Edoardo Albert, was a 3: "an extremely fortunate number, implying creative energy, brilliance, liveliness, versatility, glamour and a natural attraction for both money and the opposite sex".[74] I started calling myself Edoardo; sadly, neither money nor girls were attracted in consequence. Not daunted – and it was not a sequence in any case – I dealt out the major and minor arcana, twisted and let fall the divining sticks to consult the *I Ching* (not having access to the preferred yarrow stalks, I found the sticks from a Pik-a-Styk made a good alternative), and learned how to cast horoscopes (a major operation in the days before computers, involving planetary tables and a great number of pencil-and-paper calculations). Even in my teens I was too stiff to adopt the lotus position – just sitting cross-legged had been an ankle strainer at school – but I forced myself down into as close an approximation of the pose as I could manage and listened to my breath and attempted to shut down the run of my thoughts. I had little success, until one afternoon, when

---

73 Cavendish, 1974, page 159.
74 Cavendish, 1974, page 159.

I picked up a new book, sat down on the floor in my room, and opened it to its epigraph:

> My Beloved is the mountains, the
> solitary wooded valleys, strange
> islands...silent music

and went into the dark.

Of the next quarter-hour, I have no memory.

I, slowly, came to myself, still sitting upon the swirly 1970s carpet in my bedroom. I did not know where I had been, nor where I had gone – I do not know now. But my life was changed; now, and forever, I sought those strange islands and that silent music.

CHAPTER 7

LIKE SHINING FROM SHOOK FOIL

It was 1982. I was nineteen and sitting in a van parked on a road in Pinner and I was as unhappy as only a nineteen-year-old can be. Belief in God had crept up on me, sneaking in through the openings made by my interest in the occult. After all, if there were more things in heaven and earth than could be encompassed in that flat philosophy, then some of the other strands of my young belief could be pulled together: magic, fantasy, wonder. Could a horizontal world of material things encompass even a single tree?

We had moved house, from one suburb to another. Until I was ten we'd lived off the Archway Road, in a three-storey house my parents had scrimped and saved to buy; it had cost them £3,600 (yes, you are reading that right). But the house came with a controlled tenant: up at the top, occupying the second floor and seldom descending from it was old Mrs Boots. As a controlled tenant, she had absolute tenure of her flat, and the rent, now paid to us, was set. Unfortunately, it had been set in 1948. My parents had, in effect, bought two-thirds of a house – which was why the house was cheap enough for them to afford. Just. Mrs Boots had her cooker on the landing between her two rooms and there was no more chance of moving that than there was of moving her.

To afford the mortgage, my parents rented out the first-floor rooms, leaving the ground floor of our own house for the four of us. The tenants were mostly young women, attracted by the homely atmosphere of living in a house with a family, and my brother and I made friends with many of them. In memory, most were nurses, or student nurses, but there was one exception: Mr Kaseem.

Mr Kaseem was Nigerian. My parents, when they had first married, had spent many days tramping fruitlessly from one advertised bedsit to another. "Oh, yes, Mrs Albert, we have a nice, clean room, ideal for a young couple," the landlord or landlady would say when they rang from a call box, the coins clicking in as the money ran down, only for the door to open and the welcoming face to stiffen when it registered my father's brown skin.

"It's taken." And the door would close.

An old Quaker lady – Auntie Dorothy for ever after – took them in finally, giving them a room in her house in Kentish Town. Even after my brother and I were born, and we moved out because the room had become too small, Auntie Dorothy remained a family friend. She was a spinster, with the customary fondness for cats, and she gave my parents a clock that they have still, while my father would pop round to repair her television and radio whenever they broke down.

In such a context, owning their own house, even if it came with a controlled tenant, became a major consideration for my parents, and in 1965 they had finally saved – and I mean saved: not a single penny was spent upon themselves beyond the absolute necessities – enough to buy 25 Davenant Road.

So when Mr Kaseem came looking to rent a room, there was no stiffening of face – although with a name like Kaseem and a thick Nigerian accent, there wasn't much doubt when he rang that the face at the door would be black – and he took one of the first-floor rooms.

It did not work out. Of all the tenants we had, he was the only one my parents asked to leave. He did so with ill grace and muttered threats, which, naturally, we did not take seriously. However, it turned out Mr Kaseem's threats were serious.

A week later the doorbell rang in the evening, unexpectedly, and my father went to answer it. My mother, not sure why, followed after him, just in time to grab his arm as Mr Kaseem attempted to pull him out of the house – so that the three friends Mr Kaseem had brought with him could start throwing punches too. My mother held one arm, Mr Kaseem pulled the other – my father an unlikely object of tug-of-war – while Mr Kaseem's friends tried to grab hold. Coming to see what was going on, my mother screamed at my brother and me to hide – and I did, under the bed. My brother, braver than I, tried to help, grabbing Father's leg and holding on. The shouts and screams drew neighbours from their houses and, from the other first-floor flat, Rita, a student nurse from Ireland, and her boyfriend. (My parents had told Rita in no uncertain terms that her boyfriend could visit but under no circumstances was he to stay the night – they took in lodgers, they did not run a bawdy house.)

Other hands joined the struggle and my father, enraged, shook off his assailants. It was only my mother's restraining hand that stopped him pursuing Mr Kaseem and his friends as they made their escape.

It was in this context that, when they had saved enough money to buy a house unencumbered with a controlled tenant, my parents moved out, rather than in. They could have afforded a similar, three-storey Victorian terrace house closer in to town, but Islington was such a slum they didn't even think of moving there. So, in common with all the Italian and Asian immigrants, we moved outwards – to a nice, 1930s, semi-detached house on the border of Palmers Green and Wood Green. The houses had followed the Piccadilly Line as it bored through London's chalk underlayer, fanning out from the Charles Holden-designed stations that united form and function in a manner that still calms even today's rushed commuters and must have delighted those first commuters, newly liberated from the smoke of London to live amid the parks and greenery of Metroland.

We lived at 90 Norfolk Avenue for ten years. When we moved in, the heating was still coal-fired and the coal man would call round in his big, soot-marked lorry every week to unload bags of coal for the coal bunker in the back garden. I can propose, from personal experience, an inflexible law of fire lighting: the ease with which a coal fire lights is inversely proportional to how cold and wet the person trying to light the fire is. In winter, ice formed on the inside of the bedroom windows as the night's exhalation froze, and clothes, left carefully at the end of the bed before sleeping, were pulled inside the blankets to be changed into while pulling the bedclothes tight to retain the sleeping warmth. It occurs to me that I might be a member of the last generation to experience this; and the tightness of family life, when all the warmth was confined to one room with a burning fire and all the rest of the house was a fridge, with only the kitchen offering an alternative source of warmth, at least while meals were being cooked.

And then, the spread, the expansion, the sheer warmth, when the men came and laid in the pipes and put up the radiators. Central heating. I retired to my room and my books. Would I have become what I have if we had remained huddled before the fire? For good and ill, I doubt it.

Alone with my loves, I found my way back towards God – and thoroughly miserable that made me.

We moved again. To Arnos Grove, and a house left unoccupied for ten years. We were rich now, or seemed so by our standards, for my father, at the age of fifty, had started in business on his own, repairing televisions and the new-fangled video recorders for his old employers, John Lewis. And my brother and my mother and I all helped, with varying degrees of interest and commitment. My brother, relieved to be finally shot of school, took to the work with ease, learning his way around circuit boards and valves (yes, when we started there were still plenty of televisions around that used the old, beautiful thermionic valves). My mother left her job as a merchandiser – putting Brown & Paulson baby food out on the shelves of supermarkets – to run the office side of things, answering the phone, making out invoices, ordering spares. And I, the young intellectual, the boy with the book, rode along in the van as muscle. Those televisions were heavy. And, another invariable rule: the higher people lived in a block of flats – particularly one where the lift had broken – the bigger and heavier the television they owned.

I was not a happy young man.

Set upon academic tramlines leading to a career in science (my mother, naturally, wanted me to be a doctor but scientist sounded a reasonable second best), I had derailed myself with books. Determined on becoming a physicist and unlocking the secrets of the universe, and earning myself the third and vacant place beside Isaac Newton and Albert Einstein, I'd made the mistake of getting interested in, first, the occult and then, fatally, philosophy.

Philosophy may be the love of wisdom, but in the teenage boy it is the path to madness. Never is the mind so plastic, so impressionable, so ready to make intuitive leaps and imaginative associations – there is a reason the greatest scientists generally make their most groundbreaking discoveries when barely old enough to shave. If I had just kept on the tracks I'd set for myself, I would have gone straight on to university after leaving school at eighteen – admittedly totally naïve but at least set firmly upon habits of study that would have seen me through my degree. But I had discovered Plato. I followed him, struck with teenage wonder, out of the Cave and into... well, I wasn't really sure. A world that was wider and stranger than I had believed, a world where, maybe, elves and dwarves and dragons might have a home as well as photons, electrons, and protons, but a world that, on a personal level, had drawn down to sitting on the floor in my bedroom and living only in books. You see, I'd made the mistake of deciding to take a year between leaving school and going to university. I was going to write a book; I was going to wander and wonder and travel and get a job; I was going to get a girlfriend. That was what I was going to do. What I did was sit in my room.

I tried to write a book. The book meandered through a couple of hundred pages before boring itself to a stop. The job was tried, and left, the travels never started. And, rather unsurprisingly, no girls showed any interest in a tongue-tied, spot-ridden teenager whose idea of conversation was giving a lecture on Plato's archetypes. Mind you, that would have been an improvement; as it was, I never actually managed to pluck up the courage to talk to any real, live girls.

There is, I suspect, a larger percentage of lifelong bachelors among philosophers than any other branch of academia (with the possible exception of mathematicians), for a very good reason: while there may not, strictly, be any more to life than ontology, this is not necessarily best brought up on a first date. Nor, indeed, my life as a werewolf (if you ever read this, Inari, I am sorry).

I was miserable, and doing nothing. My parents and brother were working all the hours they had, and some they had not, setting up the business. It was taken as read that I would not be joining this – I'd been the academic one all along – but then I, er, dropped out of university.

I'd had my year off. For me, it was a year out, a grey hole in memory, but such was the pallor it cast that when I eventually started on my degree – in physics and philosophy – I could not continue. The press of people, the shock of contact was all too much. First, I stopped going to lectures, wandering around the university. Then I stopped going to the university at all, and wandered the streets. Then I stopped even doing that, and stayed at home.

By the time my parents found out, it was too late. I'd missed too much and I was out. To buy off their anger and disappointment, I agreed to try for medical school, but in the meantime, rather than sit at home, I agreed to help with the business.

Which was how I found myself sitting in a van in Pinner. My father had gone in to repair a television. I sat outside, to be called upon should the TV need to be taken back to our workshop (the business had expanded from the kitchen table to premises on the North Circular Road).

The radio was playing. I wound down the window. A bush, thick with overgrowing honeysuckle, hung over the pavement. The Isley Brothers were playing on the radio, and as the scent of summer filled the van, the harmonies of "Summer Breeze", and then the guitar solo that ends the song, spiralling into the sun, joined together, and the world, the world was still, listening. Everything, everything balanced upon that point; everything was listening and everything heard.

And I, I was happy, with the unreflective, natural joy that does not even realize its gladness until it is spent.

Amid the unrelenting misery of those years, those few minutes sitting in a van in, of all places, Pinner, still sparkle, offsetting the grey surrounding them.

It was a taste, a small taste no doubt but still a taste, of what I had decided I wanted: the direct experience of God. I wanted out of the Cave; I wanted to see and feel and hear clear, without the awful pig monkey of my own self-awareness sat upon my shoulder, whispering into my ear. I wanted the direct and truthful vision

171

of, well, Truth. I wanted to know, not with the sort of recursive, reflective knowledge that comes of the endless stream of words running through my mind, but to know in my blood and bones, in my bowels and gut, in my heart; knowledge as sight.

By this time, I'd read enough to know what I was after: the mystical vision of God. The fire that burst upon Blaise Pascal.

> The year of grace 1654,
> Monday, 23 November...
> From about half past ten at night until about half past midnight,
>
> FIRE.

> GOD of Abraham, GOD of Isaac, GOD of Jacob
> not of the philosophers and of the learned.
> Certitude. Certitude. Feeling. Joy. Peace.
> ... Righteous Father, the world has not known you, but I have known you.[75]

But vision had not burst upon me like Pascal's Godbomb – I had had intimations, sentiments, senses, but not more. I desired the mountains and the solitary wooded valleys, I wanted to sail to those strange islands, but the problem was simple: I lived in London. I lived in the city that had given birth to the modern world and there was a distinct lack of mountains, no solitary wooded valleys (unless you counted Highgate Wood), and definitely no strange islands.

There is, at the heart of the obscure and unspoken but deep feeling the English have for their country, a profound but understated nature mysticism. I was not English, but my reading had poured some of that nostalgic homelonging into my soul: the River and even the Wild Wood in *The Wind in the Willows*,

---

75 Source: http://www.users.csbsju.edu/~eknuth/pascal.html (accessed 9 August 2015).

Hampshire's *Watership Down*, the Shropshire hills of the *Lone Pine* books and, most of all, the Shire. The natural mysticism of the English is nature mysticism. God walks amid meads and daffodils, on mountains green and amid pleasant pastures. That was the path I wanted to take – indeed, I'd been given a glimpse of what it brought during my vision from Pinner – but, but... The first fact of London's geography is the river and the second the people: the overwhelming, never-ending mass of people. God wasn't going to be found in sylvan groves – not when Metroland had extinguished the dells and copses of Middlesex and, in the end, consigned the county itself to solitary cricketing remembrance. But others through London's long past had met God, face to face, amid the streaming, teeming hordes and, of these, the foremost was, undoubtedly, William Blake.

That judgement would come as a surprise to his contemporaries. They, even the few who appreciated his work, thought he was mad. It didn't help that he was the son of a hosier. Blake's formal education amounted to being taught to read and write – he left school at ten. His informal education had begun six years earlier, when God looked in through the window. The four-year-old William screamed. A few years later, a slightly older Blake saw in Peckham Rye "a tree filled with angels, bright angelic wings bespangling every bough like stars".[76]

There are people like this, who walk in vision. Whether we choose to accept or ignore the reality of those visions is up to us, but it depends, reasonably enough, on the life evidence of the person in question. Blake saw visions, and denounced the rich and the powerful, while remaining faithful to his wife and working hard to support them; and during this time he produced one of the greatest bodies of artistic and poetic work in English history:

---

76   Bentley and Bentley, 1995, pages 36–37.

if this be the product of madness, let the visions come, say I. But these visions are not always benign and even Blake, who normally defined his very idea of himself by what he saw, yet might bewail the stamp they left upon him:

> O why was I born with a different face?
> Why was I not born like the rest of my race?[77]

Others, still, are driven into madness or exile through what they see.

There was a man I visited, a couple of times, to repair his television. Let's call him John. He lived in a bedsit in Edgware, one of the Metroland suburbs of London that were built during the 1930s as the underground lines ate into Middlesex, covering its fields and copses with rows and crescents of semi-detached, Tudor-style houses – I live in one myself. John rented a room in one of these, but it was not like other rooms. John was bearded – two decades before beards became hipster badges – and in his thirties. The walls of his room were covered with holy pictures and photographs, in particular images of the Sacred Heart (for those not raised upon Catholic devotions, those are the slightly weird images of Jesus with his heart exposed and red in the middle of his chest), and of Padre Pio. St Pio of Pietrelcina was a Capuchin monk, stigmatic, visionary, and miracle worker who lived in the Gargano Peninsula of Italy – the bit that sticks out like the spur of the Italian boot – from 1887 to 1968 and who has, judged according to a quick travelling count of pictures, photos, and statues on display in southern Italy, overtaken Jesus as God's right-hand man and is poised on the shoulder of the Blessed Virgin Mary. If this all reads as just too shocking for Protestant sensibilities, honestly, don't sweat it. It really doesn't mean Catholics worship Mary, or Padre Pio; it's more a quite

---

77 Keynes, 1970, page 65.

calculated Mediterranean response to the supernatural economy: whom should I go to in order to present my petition? In this, it bears a thoroughgoing resemblance to the Italian national economy, particularly in the south, where connections, preferably familial but anything will do, are crucial for landing positions, jobs, and contracts. And no, this is not nearly as corrupt as it sounds, but a rational response to a state apparatus so creaking and incompetent that the only way to achieve an end is via the clear channels of obligation rather than the clogged arteries of governmental bureaucracy.

Entering John's room was like walking into the mind of a religious obsessive, but the man himself was kind and thoughtful. He offered me tea as I worked on his television – always a sure way to win favour with a workman – and then, when I asked about the pictures, he began to talk; slowly, hesitantly at first, and then in torrents of words.

John had been a monk, a novice in the same order that Padre Pio belonged to, but when it came time for his final vows, he had been asked to leave the monastery. The monks did not want him. He saw too much, and too often, and he burned with it. Such a fire makes for fascinating conversations with visiting repairmen and an uncomfortable community. They cast him out. Now John worked shifts in a local factory making biscuits, and saw visions there, and held his tongue, lest he be cast out again. He would return each night alone to his room walled with images of the one man who might have been able to speak, as one who knows, to John. But Padre Pio was dead, and though sometimes John saw him too, the Capuchin spoke not to him, but wept with him, as they maintained their lonely suburban vigil of prayer.

It turned out that John, although no longer a monk, still kept monastic hours: rising at 3 a.m. to pray through the dark watches of the night for the world that slept unheeding around his solitary cell.

Was John mad? He saw visions, he heard voices – even his fellow monks had cast him out. Yet he was still able to work – just. There had been a previous couple of jobs where visions had broken upon him unexpectedly and left him helpless, gasping, and entirely unable to screw tops on bottles or check the cherry atop a cherry Bakewell. And he lived independently, unsupported by state or church. Was John mad? I did not think so, although meeting him, I began to realize the price, in loneliness and derision, the vision of God might demand.

William Blake paid much of that price too, but at least he was blessed with kindly and understanding parents. James and Catherine Blake were Dissenters, although of which sect is not known: they were buried in Bunhill Fields, the graveyard reserved for Nonconformists. The mortal remains of their most famous son would later join them there. Although the exact site of William's body has been lost, a plaque shows roughly where he lies.

While Blake's academic schooling ended when he was ten, James and Catherine Blake well knew their third child was no run-of-the-mill boy and they supported him as best they could: displaying his youthful drawings and poems on the walls in their house, enrolling him at the Henry Pars Drawing School on the Strand for four years, and even giving him an allowance to buy old prints. The dealers came to know this earnest, pugnacious, strange boy well, and did him deals when no other buyer was in prospect. When his studies at the Drawing School ended, the fourteen-year-old Blake, rather than entering one of the newly created art schools, was apprenticed to James Basire, engraver. His indenture is still kept at Stationers' Hall, London.

There's no reason to doubt the explanation Blake later gave a friend for this: the cost of coming under the tutelage of a professional artist being too high, Blake asked his father to secure him the cheaper post of apprentice engraver.

From Basire, Blake learned the patience and hard, physical skills necessary for the engraver: through the rest of his life, the knives and copper, the dyes and presses and rollers that were the engraver's stock in trade were his constant companions.

Unschooled, Blake taught himself. Apprentices were expected to work twelve-hour days with only Sunday off, but the youth managed to immerse himself in words as well as pictures: echoes of and allusions to Shakespeare and Jonson, Milton and Spenser pepper his work. Blake was no fan of the newfangled use of oil in painting that had been pioneered by the likes of Rubens and Rembrandt, decrying its smudging of line and blurring of outline. Look at one of his engravings, say *The Ancient of Days* where Urizen, bending double, geometrizes the world into being. The figure of Urizen stands in sharp, engraved relief from the background. Thus is it in Blake's art and mind: the particular, blazing in the light of his imaginative vision, highlighted against the general background – for everything that lives is holy, and all that lives in Blake's art is holy, its life a gift of God's secret fire.

Such a young man was not likely, after seven years' apprenticeship, to simply knuckle down to earning a living as an engraver, turning the pictures of others into mass-produced prints for a newly wealthy middle class looking to ape its aristocratic models but without the financial means to buy original works of art. Prints were signals of aspiration and arrival, saying that those with taste and money to display them had moved well above the common mass of men, even if they were not (yet) among the titled. The young Blake applied to the Royal Academy Schools, submitting a drawing and testimonial. He was accepted, and began the six years of training. Tuition was free and in the evenings, so the students could support themselves by working during the day. The Royal Academy Schools had only been going for eleven years when Blake joined, but already the signal desire of its founders – to found a school of English art to match those of the past – was showing signs of success. Not only were notable artists being produced, but the English, who had heretofore shown not the slightest interest in daubs of paint stuck up on walls, were beginning to patronize galleries and exhibitions and, more importantly, to stick their hands into their wallets to pay for new ones.

While visiting relatives in Battersea, the young Blake met Catherine Boucher, the daughter of a market gardener and the woman who was to become his wife. Blake had already had one marriage proposal turned down but it was as well. It is unlikely that any other woman would have supported and encouraged, renewed and restored Blake as she did, even though, as evidenced by the "X" she inscribed in the marriage register, she came to him illiterate. Unlettered Catherine might have been, but she was not unintelligent, and she learned to print and colour her husband's work. Upon his deathbed, Blake drew a final portrait of Catherine, telling his wife: "You have ever been an angel to me." Would that we all might say the same as death nears: I think I will.

Although Blake was to become, in effect, an exile at home later in life, at this time he moved among and heard much of contemporary London thought. In particular, he accepted the idea, made fashionable by the passion for antiquities, that before and alongside Christianity, there was a body of ancient wisdom, passed on in the writings of such figures as Hermes Trismegistus, Plato, Paracelsus, and Jacob Boehme, that was almost another revelation. Indeed, during his apprenticeship, Blake had lived opposite Freemasons' Hall – and the Masons believed themselves to be the inheritors of knowledge held from before the Flood.

Blake's father died in 1784 and William moved with Catherine into the house next to his mother, at 27 Broad Street. With his fellow apprentice to James Basire, James Parker, Blake set up a print shop, the two men living with their wives above the shop. They had timed their venture well, for print-making was expanding rapidly in London, and business was good enough for William and Catherine to move round the corner, to 28 Poland Street, into a four-storey house with a basement.

This would have been the ideal time for Catherine to fall pregnant, but she never did. None of William's siblings produced children, suggesting an inherited infertility; the thought of Blake as a father, playing with the angels playing with his firstborn, remains sadly unfulfilled. Of all his siblings he was closest to his young brother Robert, helping him also to enrol at the Royal Academy Schools. But Robert fell ill. William tended him through his last weeks, not leaving his side and barely sleeping for his final fortnight upon this earth, until "[a]t the last solemn moment, the visionary eyes beheld the released spirit ascend heavenward through the matter-of-fact ceiling 'clapping its hands for joy'".[78]

But that was not the end of Blake's intercourse with Robert for, thirteen years later, he wrote: "with his spirit I converse daily & hourly in the Spirit & see him in my remembrance in the regions of my Imagination. I hear his advice & even now write from his Dictate."[79]

His brother dead, Blake slept as one dead, for three days and three nights.

Blake was engraver, poet, and painter: three very different skills. He excelled at each; how could he combine them? In the end, his brother told him. His dead brother. William related that Robert Blake appeared to him in vision and imagination and told him what to do. Having mastered the process, Blake was able to print his own books on his own printing press, combining pictures and words through the medium of engraving. Blake kept the first works he completed by his new method with him throughout his life, printing, colouring, and binding them until his death, for in

78 Gilchrist, 1907, page 58.
79 Keynes, 1970, page 15.

them he achieved a unity of thought and art and vision that he had been seeking all along.

The titles of these two little series are telling: "All Religions Are One" and "There is No Natural Religion". Reading them, as a youth, I had the breadth of background to wish the first true while lacking the depth of education to understand what was meant by the latter. A child of immigrants, I wanted all religions to be one, particularly since I could claim a fair slice of them in my family's past. Here was one of England's great poets and artists saying what I hoped. I bought a poster of *The Ancient of Days* and stuck it on my wall.

Blake, with his new method of creating word and image, of inscribing word in metal as God carved the tablets of Law he gave to Moses, was becoming as much prophet as poet, at least in his mind. Railing against the dry, mechanistic world of Newton and the Deists, positing their God as a slightly more efficient engineer, setting the cogs in motion and then letting the clockwork run, Blake offered his visions and his images, bathed in spiritual light.

The body, in art and life, was the vehicle of that light and had once been unsullied and pure. Blake, in common with some of the radical sects of the time, saw in the prelapsarian nakedness of Adam and Eve the purity of mankind's original, unfallen state and, never one to do things by halves, set about copying them. William and Catherine Blake had moved to Lambeth at the end of 1790, setting up home at 13 Hercules Buildings, Westminster Bridge. Hard though it is now to imagine, Lambeth was then a bucolic place, with open fields visible from their house, and the ponds, streams, and bogs of the original marsh the haunt of birds and little creatures. The Blakes were doing well enough financially to afford a house with a garden, front and back, and these gardens were a delight to them, although the neighbours seem to have been of different mind. While reciting passages from *Paradise Lost*, William and Catherine Blake, in order to get into the characters of Adam and Eve when they spoke in the poem, would sit in the garden of Hercules Buildings in prelapsarian dress: that is, completely naked.

As balance to the apparent innocence and naivety of this scene, think on Blake's temper, and his prickly if uncertain sense of self-worth. He believed himself to be poet and prophet, an artist working at the highest level, but the only person who unreservedly agreed with this opinion was his wife – his originally illiterate wife. It took peculiar, almost maniacal levels of self-belief to keep working with so little public recognition, particularly since Blake's early career had suggested that public acclaim might be forthcoming, only for it all to dribble and slide away throughout his life. Every new work or even his invention of relief printing, which he had been sure would make his fortune, came to naught. Blake could either give up and devote himself to commercial printing – he was a fine craftsman and could have amply supported himself and his wife this way – or continue in his lonely groove, etching out visions that no one wanted to see. He chose the latter, and maybe could have done no other. As a young man, he was on the fringe of various fashionable societies, where people as eminent as Henry Fuseli, Tom Paine, Mary Wollstonecraft, and William Godwin met, talked, and dined; his direct speech first bought him entry and then excluded him from such company. Unanimity and accord was still the end point towards which polite conversation aimed, although as the eighteenth century neared its end such ideals were withering before the realization that there were permanent differences that could not be occluded, "parties" that could not be reconciled. At first, Blake must have been good value at table, but he soon tired of the badinage and raillery associated with these gatherings. In all likelihood, the literary great and good of the time probably divested themselves of a man of lower social class who insisted upon the truth of his opinions with a fierceness that brooked no debate.

That fierceness could take physical form. The most notorious episode occurred when the Blakes moved to Felpham in Sussex between 1800 and 1803. Blake was forty-three and his career was going nowhere, but he had found a patron and friend in the writer William Hayley, who suggested he move to Felpham, where Hayley had his home. The move went well initially, but Blake began to chafe under Hayley's well-meaning but patronizing patronage, and resolved to return to London. The Blakes had still not left in August when a soldier, John Scolfield, came into the garden. The gardener had invited him, but Blake did not know this, and invited the dragoon to leave. When Scolfield refused, and words were exchanged, Blake, despite being the older and shorter man, physically ejected him from the garden, but the argument continued down the road to the Fox Inn, where what passed between Blake and Scolfield was witnessed by a number of people. Although indicative of Blake's temper, and his fearlessness, the matter would normally have ended there. But Scolfield later charged Blake with damning the king of England and making seditious comments in favour of the French. With England at war with Napoleonic France, and in fear of invasion upon the very coast where the Blakes were living, this charge was serious: Blake was summoned to appear before court. Given the republican views espoused in Blake's works and his initial joy at the French Revolution, the idea that Blake, in the heat of fury, might have called curses down upon the king or supported the enemies of the soldier in front of him doesn't seem at all unlikely, but when the case came before court Blake's lawyer, and his character witnesses, were sufficient to see him acquitted.

Blake saw visions of eternity, but he saw them clothed in the smoke and grime of London: he was a poet and prophet of the city and, after three years away, he had to return to it. He wrote, after his return: "I can alone carry on my visionary studies in London unannoy'd, & that I may converse with my friends in Eternity, See Visions, Dream Dreams & prophecy & speak Parables..."[80]

The Blakes moved into a house at 17 South Molton Street, Mayfair – it was not nearly as fancy an address then as it is now – and declined into a life of obscurity that flirted on the edges of the real, abject, not-enough-money-to-eat poverty that then afflicted Londoners who were down on their luck. Blake, an accomplished engraver, should have had enough work to keep them, particularly since there were no children to feed, but he complained: "Every Engraver turns away work ... Yet no one brings work to me."[81] In part, this seems to be because Blake had acquired a reputation for being late with his engravings: visitors reported finding him lost, rapt in vision, when he should have been grinding copper plates or rolling out prints. While at Lambeth, the Blakes had been sufficiently wealthy to be worth robbing. In Mayfair, and for most of the rest of their lives, it would have been a desperate and disappointed thief who broke into their home, unless he had an unexpected appreciation for unsold copies of Blake's "illuminated books".

What is an artist to do when public and peers turn away? The obvious course is something different, and Blake did attempt that at various points. But whenever he tried to follow public taste, his efforts were rebuffed, the subsequent humiliation all the greater for the sense that he had sold his gifts to curry favour.

Change, then? Admit the truth espoused by the wallets of his contemporaries and give up? To us, now, with the benefit of a retrospect denied him, of course the answer is no. But we are talking about a lifetime of obscurity, of decade after decade of work done, and ignored, save by his faithful wife – and the value of her approbation must surely have gnawed at Blake. In "Auguries

---

80   Keynes, 1970, page 55.
81   Essick, 2004.

of Innocence", the poem where prophecy and lyric come together into their most perfect alignment, Blake answers doubt with all the force at his command:

He who mocks the infant's faith
Shall be mock'd in age and death.
He who shall teach the child to doubt
The rotting grave shall ne'er get out...

He who replies to words of doubt
Doth put the light of knowledge out...
A riddle, or the cricket's cry,
Is to doubt a fit reply...

He who doubts from what he sees
Will ne'er believe, do what you please.
If the sun and moon should doubt,
They'd immediately go out.

This was a man who had seen, and who staked his life upon what he had seen. To his great good fortune, he had a wife who believed him, yet retained sufficient managerial nous to remind him of the need for work through these thin years by placing an empty plate upon the table when there was no food to fill it, thus keeping them from the clutches of Lady Poverty.

There is a hidden penalty in growing up in an immigrant household: your parents, having grown up on different stories, don't know what to read you as a child. My parents were set upon the value of reading, but as to the content, once I could read for myself, they left me to it. Undirected, my magpie readings ranged widely but haphazardly through the classics of children's literature: I loved *The Wind in the Willows*, but never read *Winnie the Pooh*. I took the *Swiss Family Robinson* for my desert-island prototype but never walked the

strand with *Robinson Crusoe*. And I first visited Middle-earth when I
was fourteen, and went through the wardrobe in my twenties. But
there is a passage there, in *The Silver Chair*, which expresses what I
had come to believe. Puddleglum, the Marshwiggle (and if you don't
know what a Marshwiggle is, the name itself is a clue to his nature:
Eeyore without the joy), and the children, Eustace and Jill, have
been captured by the Queen of the Underworld and are being held
captive in her gloomy kingdom. The Queen lays an enchantment
upon them, making them forget the land above whence they came,
that they might think only her own shadow realm real. As the spell
takes hold, Puddleglum thrusts his hand into the fire, seeking in
pain some clearing of the mind fog, and then gives reason for his
belief, despite all doubt, all pressure, and every despair.

"One word, Ma'am," he said, coming back from the fire;
limping, because of the pain. "One word. All you've been
saying is quite right, I shouldn't wonder. I'm a chap who always
liked to know the worst and then put the best face I can on
it. So I won't deny any of what you said. But there's one thing
more to be said, even so. Suppose we *have* only dreamed, or
made up, all those things – trees and grass and sun and moon
and stars and Aslan himself. Suppose we have. Then all I can
say is that, in that case, the made-up things seem a good deal
more important than the real ones. Suppose this black pit of
a kingdom of yours *is* the only world. Well, it strikes me as a
pretty poor one. And that's a funny thing, when you come to
think of it. We're just babies making up a game, if you're right.
But four babies playing a game can make a play-world which
licks your real world hollow. That's why I'm going to stand by
the play-world. I'm on Aslan's side even if there isn't any Aslan
to lead it. I'm going to live as like a Narnian as I can even if
there isn't any Narnia. So, thanking you kindly for our supper,

if these two gentlemen and the young lady are ready, we're leaving your court at once and setting out in the dark to spend our lives looking for the Overland. Not that our lives will be very long, I should think; but that's a small loss if the world's as dull a place as you say."[82]

There is one night I remember from my childhood above all others. This was the 1970s, and the miners were on strike, and the power workers, and the dustmen. There was a three-day week, which sounds rather delightful to my adult self, and regular blackouts. It was cold, and clear, and I looked up, and saw. The city's glare drowns the stars, but with the lights out, I could see and understand for the first time what Tolkien meant when he wrote: "And thus was the habitation of the Children of Ilúvatar established at the last in the Deeps of Time and amidst the innumerable stars."[83] To my eyes, looking up at the normal London night sky, there weren't many more than could be counted on fingers and toes.

The stars came out. Staring up, I longed for *Nightfall*, when a civilization that has known only day sees, once in a thousand thousand years, the night fall and the stars come out. I understood then: we light our cities to hide from the stars. Modern civilization, with all its triviality and idols, could not long survive if, every night, we looked up into the deep.

William Blake was not trivial. Although there were hours and days, indeed months, of despair, there were consolations beyond understanding in his life. Speaking of those peers who, held high in contemporary esteem, patronized him, Blake said, "They pity me, but 'tis they are the just objects of pity, I possess my visions and peace. They have bartered their birthright for a mess of pottage."[84]

---

82 Lewis, 1976, pages 156–57.
83 Tolkien, 1977, page 22.
84 Spurgeon, 2004.

What's more, the spiritual vision that had sustained him in his youth, but had withdrawn somewhat as he entered adulthood, returned full force as he neared his fifties, and remained with him until the end of his life.

William Blake died on 12 August 1827. In his last years, he had been adopted by a group of young artists who revered him; such approbation meant a great deal to a man so long ignored. Another artist, John Linnell, had become friends with Blake in 1818 and worked hard to support him, providing him with commissions that supplied a small but steady income.

Blake's health worsened from the spring of 1825. He nearly died in the winter of 1826/27, reporting that he had been "near the Gates of Death & have returned very weak & an Old Man feeble & tottering, but not in Spirit & Life not in The Real Man The Imagination which Liveth for Ever".[85]

On the day of his death, Blake turned to the one person who had supported him through all the years of labour and trial. "Stay, Kate! keep just as you are – I will draw your portrait – for you have ever been an angel to me."[86] The drawing done, Blake began to sing hymns, telling his weeping wife, "My beloved! they are not mine. No! they are not mine."[87]

A friend, present that day, wrote shortly afterwards that Blake:

died on Sunday Night at 6 Oclock in a most glorious
manner. He said He was going to that Country he had all
His life wished to see & expressed Himself Happy hoping
for Salvation through Jesus Christ – Just before he died His
Countenance became fair – His eyes brighten'd and He burst
out in Singing of the things he Saw in Heaven.[88]

---

85   Blake, 1982, page 783.
86   Bentley, 1969, page 502.
87   Gilchrist, 1907, page 381.
88   Bentley, 1969, pages 346–47.

By the account she later gave, not even death separated William from Catherine Blake. She maintained her husband's business, consulting with him on all things, despite his temporary incapacity through death, a process made easier since Blake would come and visit her each day, and advise her on business. Catherine Blake died four years after her husband, calling out to him that she would be with him soon.

Blake had seen, and I believed.

To see a world in a grain of sand
And a heaven in a wild flower,
Hold infinity in the palm of your hand,
And eternity in an hour.[89]

---

89 Blake, 1972, page 333.

CHAPTER 8

SUFI'S WORLD

The late 1970s were not a great time to go looking for God. The 1980s weren't much of an improvement. The thing was, I'd got as far as agreeing that God did, in fact, exist, but... then what? How did I go about finding him – or Him as I had started to capitalize in my mind? Of course, my first recourse was books. I read: *The Cloud of Unknowing*; *The Varieties of Religious Experience*; *Memories, Dreams, Reflections*; *Songlines* – the sort of magpie list you'd expect from an untutored mind picking the shiny covers from bookshops. The only reason I didn't fit in *Zen and the Art of Motorcycle Maintenance* was my complete failure as a bike rider, culminating in a tumble into a nettle bed while attempting to learn how to stop the damn thing properly.

It wasn't helped by the lack of good bookshops at the time; even in London, there was only really Foyles and Watkins: the former still stuck firmly in the Soviet era of retailing, the latter still reeking so much of 1960s hippies that I found myself blushing whenever I entered its peculiar fug of incense and book glue. How many people, I wonder, have been stopped from finding God by the sheer embarrassment of looking for him? Am I alone in the main reason for my hesitating to give change to beggars – we are, after all, enjoined to give to those who ask – being the possibility of being seen doing so? There should have been another outcome in the parable of the sower: the seed that fell on rich soil but was then too embarrassed to germinate.

Blast. I've just realized I'm likely doomed to hell's vestibule where, according to Dante, those people so undecided that they can't choose to be bad are blown and buffeted by an unceasing wind, reduced to whining presences unwanted even by the devil.

As far as I was concerned, I'd done my bit: I'd agreed to God's existence. Now it was his turn. Fugues after reading mystical poetry were all very well, but not much good if I couldn't remember anything that happened (for years afterwards, I kept a note of the date and time, thinking that if I was ever hypnotized, I'd ask to be taken back to that point to find out what really happened when I heard the silent music in the solitary wooded valleys below the mountains and among the strange islands).

But God, for his part, was keeping schtum. No messages, no visions, nothing beyond a sense that I ought to do something accompanied by a complete lack of knowledge as to what. I mean, I was going to Mass, but it still passed me by: whatever you've heard of the poverty of Catholic church preaching, the reality in the 1980s surpassed it. And, Protestant readers, yes I had tried reading the Bible and, apart from little bits of the Gospels, it left me cold and unmoved – as much a surprise to bookworm me as anything that's happened in my life. I tried other tacks but the Charismatic renewal that had taken off in places positively repelled me. I was a self-conscious young man; the thought of testimony, singing, or waving my hands in the air like I just didn't care in any context other than a Cameo concert was beyond me. But in fairness to Charismatics everywhere, I did wave my hands in the air, quite enthusiastically, at a Cameo gig at Wembley Arena; why I could do that for a man wearing a red codpiece but not for a man wearing a white loincloth was a question I did not consider at the time.

The answer, I decided, was work. Look, I come from an immigrant family; we imbibed the absolute belief that anything we got we'd have to work for, and I'd sat down and done that while studying for my exams. Effort, everything said, brought reward. So I set about working at God. But how?

Exercise. Or, to be precise, the spiritual exercises of St Ignatius Loyola. With money in pocket, I took the old familiar 29 bus route to Foyles (it was still in its old premises then, before it moved next door to the building that once housed St Martin's School of Art) and climbed the creaky wooden stairs to the top – if memory serves, the fourth – floor. That was the theology department, with books stuffed into shelves and piled high, and presided over by an old lady who alone seemed to have survived the regular staff purges instigated by Christina Foyle, who generally appeared to have an aversion to anyone remaining in employment for longer than a year.

As she handed me the little red book, she said that the *Spiritual Exercises* were her favourite retail item, ever since a previous customer had come in, asked for the book at the main information desk, and been directed to the Sports department. Unfortunately, the *Exercises* proved as opaque to me as if I'd been expected to work out cricket from the tea towel. The problem was, I realized, that I needed some help, some sort of guide – it was all very well for Blake, or Padre Pio, but I wasn't in that category: they had their paths up the mountain lit in neon with angels pointing the way. I was going to have to find a guide.

Great.

If there was one thing I hated, it was opening up about these matters to other people. But, having gone through the usual list of "seeker" books, I'd moved on to stuff like *Revelations of Divine Love* by Julian of Norwich, *The Imitation of Christ, Counsels on a Devout Life*, and the *Confessions* – they pretty well all agreed on the need for a spiritual director (well, apart from Augustine, whom it's pretty hard to imagine being directed anywhere by anyone except his mother).

John, the expelled monk, had put me off the idea of the monastic life – what I wanted was some way of finding God in the world, with the city and people all around me, rather than shutting myself off from everything. Besides, I had intimations of immortality, a conviction that I was put here, on this earth, to do... something. The trouble was, I did not know what. Oh, how I envied Mozart – there'd never been any doubt about what he was going to do. Yes, I'd extricated myself from the Italian/Asian my-son's-a-doctor thing by dint of being so obviously uninterested in medicine that the interview panel barely bothered to disguise their decision, but what was I going to do?

Books.

My love, my life, my mind and soul and heart.

I'd be a writer.

I was rubbish.

I had another go at writing a book. Three hundred-plus pages of single-spaced typing and the story meandered into swamp, never to emerge. I tried again, and again, and again: nothing. Through three decades, the eighties, nineties, and noughties, the sum total of my efforts was three short stories published, at the rate of one a decade. At that rate, I'd have to live a very, very long time to make a mark as a writer.

The City, though, was changing around me, and I felt it in my walking and driving. Only those people who travel the streets, particularly in the early morning when the night people have left but the day ones are yet to rise, know it well: taxi drivers, milkmen (there are still some around), postmen, delivery drivers. With my van stacked with TVs and videos, I drove the city's streets each day, its arteries growing more clogged with traffic and people, the sound and look of it changing. On the face of it, money was starting to wipe difference away, turning Wapping and Docklands, Hoxton and Brixton into variations on the same place. One after another, the old pockets of poverty in Zone 1, and then Zone 2, were bought out, and the old, the sick, the mad, and the poor moved to somewhere further out, until moneyed uniformity settled, like a drift of chocolate on a Starbucks cappuccino, upon those areas that most vocally called themselves unique. Go into a bar, a club, a café, or a house in Camden or Shoreditch, Clerkenwell or, of course, slummy old Islington and you will find everyone looking studiedly different and thinking that means they are different within.

The strange and the odd, the sacred and the secret, had moved to the suburbs, to the railway terraces laid down in the great Victorian expansion and then the curves of Tudor-faced semi-detached houses that followed the Tube lines into the fields of Middlesex and Essex, of Kent and Surrey.

Which was how I found myself walking down a long road in Hayes. Hayes was once a village, but now, taking the rule-of-M25, it lies in London. The house I was looking for was somewhere on Hatton Road, so I'd got off the tube at Hatton Cross and started walking. Turned out the house was at the other end of the road and I had a mile of sweaty walking, under the roar of planes taking off, before I got to the house: behind garden walls, tucked off a green that suggested the rural past of Bedfont before London swallowed it and Heathrow drowned it in sound.

Seeing it, I walked past, too nervous to stop, then turned and stood in front of the door.

Some doors, once opened, can never be closed again.

I knocked.

* * *

Four years earlier, I'd been a member of a book club. Like most book clubs of the time, you got a choice of three or four introductory books at greatly reduced prices as long as you promised to buy the same number of books at rather less reduced prices before leaving. I'd got my bargains and had to buy one more book before leaving for cheap pastures new and, reading the catalogue, saw something that looked interesting: according to the blurb, the book purported to show "the transcendent unity of religions" in the religions' own words.

The book was big and heavy and yellow. And through its thousand-plus pages it definitively showed, at least to my young eyes, that what I hoped was in fact true: all the world's religions really did say the same things and lead to the same destination. Like different paths up a mountain to the same summit, while the views and difficulties along the way varied, the destination was the same. And introducing each chapter, the editor had included extracts from various writers whom I had never heard of but in whose words, with their astringent championing of truth and beauty, I found a thrilling counterpoint to the wishy-washy vacillations of the time. It was as if I'd stumbled into a secret garden of knowledge. Who were these men? Their names were strange, almost magical: Ananda Coomaraswamy, René Guénon, Frithjof Schuon, Marco Pallis, Lord Northbourne, Titus Burkhardt, Martin Lings.

I started scouring the shelves of Foyles and Watkins, looking for titles by them, and started finding one or two. Although the writers were different, the tone, the sobriety, and the message were the same: the transcendent unity of religions, the decline into modernity, the ugliness of the present world, and the discarded tradition that had formed the framework of all previous civilizations, including our own before the Renaissance.

This was in the days before the internet, before everything being available at a click. To find books like these, I had to visit bookshops and send off to small publishers for clumsily typed book lists. I soon realized that most of these books were published by Perennial Books, Pates Manor, Bedfont, Middlesex. So, I wrote to the publisher. And the publisher wrote back, inviting me to visit.

So, I found myself poised outside the door, hand raised.

I knocked.

The door opened.

Some doors, once opened, can never be closed again.

* * *

The Victorian and Edwardian eras were the heyday of clubs and societies, occult circles and spiritual groups, but there was a renewal of these interests in the 1930s, the last fling of the imperial dream, when an extraordinary crop of travellers, explorers, and seekers set out into worlds that were soon to end. Think of Patrick Leigh Fermor's odyssey on foot from the Hook of Holland to Constantinople; Wilfred Thesiger among the Danakil in Ethiopia and then, just after the Second World War, crossing the Empty Quarter before oil money destroyed the land and culture there; Robert Byron; Peter Fleming; and Evelyn Waugh. Eton and Magdalen colleges in particular seemed to specialize in dangerously beautiful and reckless young men who could, apparently without effort, turn their hands from writing to photography to wartime exploits, in between mixing with every level of society, domestic and foreign.

But the fearlessness and openness that characterized these travellers also manifested itself in the inner realm: with translations and travel opening up the world and its cultures, people again started to investigate the traditions and religions of the East – with the East starting from somewhere around the Balkans. For the English, the natural point of exploration was India, but for the French-speaking world it was North Africa.

* * *

I went through the door into a new world.

These writers I'd been reading: I had sensed, behind the words and beliefs they shared, something else, some further bond. It was more than just a group of men who thought the same: there was a communion.

Going through that door in Bedfont, I was still not sure what I would find. The woman who met me was kind in a formal, slightly interrogative way, as if she was looking for something in me. For my part, I was just going to the book source, the publisher that published the books and journals I'd started devouring. We had tea – in the years to come, there would always be tea – and she told me that her husband, Francis Clive-Ross, had recently died and she had taken on the task of running Perennial Books. Would I like another cup of tea and, by the way, if I wanted to write to any of the authors she published, she would be happy to forward the letter.

Would I?

Yes.

For me, at this time they seemed like the return to this earth of Plato and Boethius. I had read as many of their books as I could find, but among this school, three names seemed clearly pre-eminent: René Guénon, Ananda Coomaraswamy, and Frithjof Schuon. I learned from Mrs Clive-Ross that Guénon and Coomaraswamy were dead, but Frithjof Schuon was alive. Getting home, I paused over the typewriter, thinking what I wanted to ask him. All the questions of faith and knowledge and religion whirled in my mind, refusing to settle, until I settled on one: what must I do to be saved?

I sent the letter to Mrs Clive-Ross and… nothing. No reply.

But as I waited, while in my favourite place – the local library – I pulled an edition of *Who's Who* from the shelf and started thumbing through it, marvelling at the strange combination of the eminent and the soon to be forgotten within its pages, when I chanced upon an entry for another of the writers I had been reading. Turned out Martin Lings, once the keeper of Oriental Manuscripts at the British Museum, lived in a small town in Kent, and his entry in *Who's Who* gave his address. So, cutting out the middlewoman, I wrote to him as well.

Martin Lings wrote back almost immediately, suggesting that I visit him at his home, since such matters were better spoken of. While the day of meeting wound round, the postman dropped a letter through our door. The return address, on the back, said it came from Frithjof Schuon and the address was given as Bloomington, Indiana.

Indiana?

I wasn't even sure where that was. Looking it up in an atlas, it turned out to be one of the United States, and Bloomington a little town in what looked like Hicksville. It looked about as promising a location as Croydon. What was a man like Frithjof Schuon doing living there?

Oh, and the answer to my question?

Pray.

The man who prays cannot be lost.

A few days later I drove to Westerham in Kent and turned up a road signposted for Chartwell, Winston Churchill's home, before branching down a quiet, deep, almost tree-enclosed lane that was as much green tunnel as open road. Parking, I stopped for a nerve-fuelled cigarette, then walked on to the address I had been given and stood in front of it.

It seemed, to my suburban eyes, the quintessential English cottage, with sprays of flowers spilling from the tiny front garden onto the quiet road.

I rang the bell.

The door opened.

I went in.

In writing this book, I realize that, in some ways, I never went out again.

* * *

In 1930, René Guénon sailed to Egypt.

He was a Frenchman, a philosopher, a traditionalist, a man who saw the whole of the great modern experiment as a disastrous falling away from the spiritual foundations of the world. He had emerged from, and previously much dabbled in, the occult underworld that flourished in Belle Époque France, having been a member of various theosophical, gnostic, and Masonic groups while researching and writing on Hinduism, and particularly the school of Hindu religious thought known as Advaita Vedanta. Advaita Vedanta is the most rigorously non-dualist of the Eastern schools of philosophy, proposing an identity between Atman – the self or soul – and Brahman – the ultimate reality, the cause of all that does not, itself, ever change.

In Egypt, René Guénon, the Frenchman, the Orientalist, the occultist and erstwhile Catholic, entered Islam. Or rather, as he later wrote, he had "moved into" it: "whoever understands the unity of traditions... is necessarily... 'unconvertible' to anything".[90] For René Guénon was the first, and key, proponent of the "transcendent unity of religions", although the phrase itself came later, being coined as the title of a book by the man who would come to take Guénon's place as the main exponent of Traditionalist views, Frithjof Schuon.

Why did Guénon become a Muslim? By all accounts, in Egypt he led an orthodox life, marrying an Egyptian woman and carrying

---

90 Sedgwick, 2004, page 77.

out the religious duties expected of a Muslim, but his writing and thought still used Hindu doctrines, and especially Advaita Vedanta, as the light by which to illuminate religious ideas and symbols. Guénon became a Muslim because of the vital importance he attached to the idea of initiation: the direct transmission of spiritual influence through the rites of a religion, or an order within that religion. As far as Guénon was concerned, initiation had died out in the West with the suppression of the Knights Templar, and while he had for a time thought that Masonic initiation was valid, the only other avenue apart from Hinduism were the Sufi orders in Islam. In Egypt, Guénon joined the Hamdiyya Shadhiliyya Sufi order, and there followed, in his writing, an increased emphasis on the need for valid initiation. Responding to this, his perplexed readers started to write to him in Egypt asking what initiation they should seek. He responded, at least in print, by exclusion. The Catholic Church, and the theosophical and neo-Hindu groups that existed in the West at that time were all, for him, without a valid initiation. Having come from a traditionalist Catholic background, Guénon did not even bother to mention any forms of Protestant Christianity. As far as Guénon was concerned, you had to be born a Hindu, and into its caste system, to be a Hindu, so that was excluded. There wasn't really much left over.

***

I was sitting, squatting rather, on a low shelf in an alcove. The windows opened onto a glorious English garden, vibrant with sky-blue delphiniums, scarlet crocosmias (the "Lucifer" variety, ironically enough), and sun-yellow heleniums.

The room, on the other hand, was as far removed from England as anywhere I'd ever seen (bar, possibly, a council flat in St John's Wood – yes, such a thing exists – whose owner had transformed the interior, through the judicious use of cladding, into a medieval castle). Reed matting, up to the level of my waist, clad the walls; red-and-yellow geometric rugs, Moroccan I later learned, covered the floor; exquisite calligraphy, in a script I didn't know but thought must be Arabic, inscribed black on a glowing gold background, was hung in modest frames on a couple of walls; and a spider plant trailed plantlets from a simple and elegant shelf. This might make the room sound ornate, but it wasn't: the house was painted simple white within and this was the background upon which the vivid reds and yellows, and occasional blues, were set: the effect was of restraint in the service of beauty.

In the alcove was a round, beautifully worked brass tray, set upon a low stand, and I sat behind it, awkwardly crossing my legs. Martin Lings, fifty-four years my senior, sat on the other side of the tray, apparently quite at ease with his legs tucked into such a position despite looking, to my young eyes, ancient, and poured the tea.

If you want to know what he looked like, think of Alec Guinness as Obi-Wan Kenobi, even down to the earth-coloured robe.

"Milk?"

"Yes, please."

He poured it into the cup first. My mother, who had a fixed obsession when I was young that I was permanently undernourished, had made tea by heating milk with tea leaves in it and adding four teaspoons of sugar. This tea did not taste like that tea.

We talked and I spoke a little of my life, while he told me something of his. It turned out he had lived in Croydon before his retirement.

After tea, Dr Lings showed me around his garden and then I left. Something had happened but, driving back home, I did not know what.

Bloomington and then Croydon. It was all getting quite strange.

* * *

In 1935 a young man, come down from Oxford having read English with C. S. Lewis as tutor, became a lecturer in Anglo-Saxon and Middle English at Vytautas Magnus University in Kaunas, Lithuania. The young man was Martin Lings, and while there he first encountered the works of René Guénon and was convinced, as he would remain to the end of his life, that he had come "face to face with the truth".[91] Despite Lewis's tutelage, the young Lings had not returned to the practice of religion while at Oxford. He once told me that, at Oxford, Lewis had said of the difference between the two of them: "I am a man for whom imagination is the dominant mental faculty, but for you, it is the intellect." For such a man, René Guénon's ideas had the force of revelation, and Lings was soon one of the many people in the Frenchman's circle of correspondents. But it was all very well accepting the idea, propounded by Guénon, that there was a common core of esoteric truth at the centre of the world's main religions; how did one go from the idea to its realization? While some of Guénon's readers were content with a purely intellectual approach to religion, Martin Lings wanted to live it as well as think it. To that end, all Guénon's public writing, and his correspondence, emphasized the need for guidance from a spiritual master. The problem was the finding of one.

* * *

Over the next year or two I visited Martin Lings on three or four occasions and, during the course of tea taken in that strange room, which I learned was called the *zawiya*, or in the garden, I slowly learned that my intimation, that more bound this school of Traditionalist writers together than simply shared ideas, was true.

They were all, or nearly all, members of a Sufi order, a tariqa.

---

91 Lings, 1998, page 15.

And the order's spiritual master, its shaykh, was Frithjof Schuon, the same Frithjof Schuon who had written to me from Bloomington. Martin Lings was the head of the order in England and, I learned, its members met fortnightly in the Kentish suburb of London, Beckenham, for what was called a *majlis*: prayer, meditation, singing, and even dancing – no whirling though – directed towards God. Or Allah.

Oh, and would I like to join?

* * *

In 1938, Martin Lings set off to find a spiritual master, leaving Lithuania and travelling south to, er, Switzerland. While he had expected to find a spiritual master amid the mountains, he'd had the Himalayas or Atlas Mountains in view rather than the Alps. But Guénon had told him where to go: Basle.

In the unlikely surroundings of this Swiss town the first functioning Sufi tariqa in the West, a tariqa composed at this time entirely of Europeans, had formed, centred upon its shaykh, Frithjof Schuon.

Born in 1907, the young Schuon had also been convinced of Traditionalist ideas by his reading of Guénon and, learning of the eminent Algerian Sufi, Shaykh Ahmad al-Alawi, sailed to Mostaghanem, where he entered al-Alawi's order, known as the Alawiyya. Schuon spent three months in Mostaghanem during which time he was, apparently, given permission to accept new members into the Alawiyya order. Returning to Europe, Schuon, according to his privately published memoirs, had his first vision, on the day of the Shaykh al-Alawi's death.

A group of some thirty or forty Traditionalists formed around Schuon, all converts to Islam but committed to the idea of the essential unity of religions. As part of that, their order remained secret. There was hardly anything unusual in that; pretty well all the mystical, occult groups flourishing in Europe in the 1930s were at least secretive if not out-and-out hidden, and Schuon's tariqa was no exception. But then, in 1937, Schuon had another vision and later said: "I woke with the certainty that I had become the shaykh".[92] The Sufi tariqa that had started as a branch of the traditional (small "t") Alawiyya order was becoming something of its own.

* * *

Would I join?

Would I become a Sufi and a Muslim, albeit one professing the essential unity of religions? This was certainly not the option I'd expected to have presented to me a few years back when I first started reading and thinking my way back towards some sort of faith.

What would I say to my parents? Not drinking wasn't really a problem – I was never much of a drinker, for the simple reason that too much alcohol, like too many drugs, simply made the room spin and me vomit – but no bacon… now that would be difficult. I'd been a vegetarian for six months, only to be broken by the smell of frying bacon.

Turned out I didn't need to tell my parents. I didn't need to tell anyone. I could keep my Islam a secret – the tariqa even licensed the discreet consumption of beer if doing so better covered one's religious tracks.

I met some of the other young men who were in the order and they were like me… children of mixed marriages and mixed heritages, the offspring of the whirling cultures of modern London: Anglo/Indian; Pakistani/Persian; Bangladeshi; and Iranian. We even looked alike, although most of them sported neat, trimmed beards.

---

92 Sedgwick, 2004, page 92.

And I liked them. I liked them a lot. High minded but with the intellectual zest and energy of the young and the committed who believe they have found the answer that everyone else is seeking, we would meet in the shisha bars of the Edgware Road and talk into the night, running abstruse metaphysical notions past rather more limited understandings of history than we realized.

I had never known like minds before. Now, the streets and cafés of my own city brought them to me and in the newly proclaimed multiculturalism of 1980s London, we saw ourselves as an intellectual elite embodying the new culture of the city. We were profoundly backward looking but our very existence in this place and time was a symbol and portent of where the city was going.

So, yes, I joined.

I became a Muslim, a Sufi, and a Perennialist – although in my mind the order was reversed.

I don't think any of my non-tariqa friends noticed.

* * *

In 1938, Martin Lings embraced Islam and became Frithjof Schuon's disciple, remaining faithful to both to the end of his life. But in 1939, a fateful year indeed, he left for Egypt to visit Guénon, only for war to break out and a visit to turn into a thirteen-year sojourn, during which time he became Guénon's personal assistant as well as teaching English at Cairo University. The Egyptian revolution in 1952 meant Lings had to leave and he returned to England.

While on leave, Martin Lings had married a childhood friend, Lesley Smalley, whom I came to know as Sayeda (an honorific title) Rabiah, the quintessential Englishwoman, kindly and acerbic in turn. On their return to Britain, they settled in Croydon – Croydon! – while Lings completed his PhD and worked as keeper of Oriental Manuscripts at the British Museum. Still, why should I find it odd that he lived in Croydon? I lived in Arnos Grove (or New Southgate, I've never quite decided which) and my years of repairing televisions had taught me that the suburbs were far, far stranger than the self-conscious exhibitionism of the city's Zone 1 metropolitans.

And while working and studying, Lings also took charge of the English branch of Schuon's Sufi order, organizing the twice-monthly meetings in Beckenham and, after his retirement, inviting about eight disciples to his house in Westerham. Tea would be taken, a lengthy walk made through the Kent countryside – Martin Lings kept up with this right into his nineties – during which he would speak to each person individually, providing counsel, advice, and just general conversation, before returning to his house and sharing a meal, followed by an hour of prayer and then silent, standing, invocation, turned towards Mecca, which lasted for up to another hour. Despite his age, I never, ever saw him flag, and even when my own legs were aching and I was beginning to sway he remained, a diminutive figure, standing in a plain Moroccan *djelleba* made of coarse wool, looking towards God.

* * *

As the only young man in the tariqa who had a car – and a van – I was often called upon to act as a taxi service for visitors. This might have been irksome, struggling through the traffic from one side of London to the other. It wasn't, because of the extraordinary people I met while acting as a taxi: from an old American who now lived in the tribal areas of Pakistan and coloured his beard red with henna, to an intense, and intensely bearded Russian (and this in the days before the fall of the Berlin Wall, when meeting a Russian was still an event), through to the memorable day when I nearly had to put an Iranian/American professor and an Arab prince into the back of a Ford transit van to get them back from Westerham.

The conversations were varied, wide ranging, and almost always memorable: I was meeting the world, eminent and low, and it was treating me as its equal. For I realized that the tariqa had members in all sorts of walks of life, from the UN's International Labour Organization through professors and academics, particularly in the fields of Islamic studies and comparative religion, to peers of the realm. One couple had been so on the beat in the 1960s that they really did go to Andy Warhol's Factory parties. Mixed in with these were the sort of young, intellectual oddities that I was myself: intense young men who really did think that the hypostases of the godhead were important and even looked it up in a dictionary to find out what it meant. (I did, actually, once use the phrase "hypostasis of the godhead" with two old, good friends who were not involved with this side of my life: they almost split their sides in laughter.)

The tariqa was unashamedly elitist in its outlook; the doctrines promulgated in the books of its members were rigorously intellectual and there was, in any case, a traditional, or Traditional, justification for such elitism in the hierarchical nature of religious civilizations, notably the caste system of Hinduism; although Islam eschews such divisions, we were supposed to be Gnostics – those who approach God through knowledge. According to the doctrines of Advaita Vedanta, Gnostics can, by their intellect, understand the other ways of approach to God – through love, duty, work, etc. – but by adding understanding, the gnostic path was supreme, for those qualified. It was a seductive idea.

But there were rumours that all was not well in the order. I heard tell of tension between the English and American branches. The English *zawiyyah*, under the guidance of Martin Lings, had accepted many young men and women over recent years who came from Muslim families. The children of immigrants like myself, they, as much as I, appreciated the chance to spend time with older, properly English people who had been in the tariqa for many years:

it was an education in manners as much as anything else, as well as an opportunity to hear tales of the past. Lings had studied with C. S. Lewis at Oxford, he'd heard J. R. R. Tolkien – my literary hero – lecture (apparently he seldom took his pipe from his mouth and was almost inaudible), and he'd gone on pilgrimage to Mecca when the only lights at night were flaming torches and the innumerable stars. We were universalists grounded in the forms of a particular religion and enjoying tutelage in the best of our home culture.

But things were different in America, in Bloomington. They had become increasingly universalist; there were strange rumours. No one quite appeared to know what was and what was not going on. And there had been disturbances in the English order as a result, which had led to many old-standing members leaving in the time before I joined, including Mrs Clive-Ross, who had first opened the door of this new world to me.

Then the news came that we were to have a visitor from America. It seemed like a chance to heal the breach. Although it was not going to be any eminent member of the order in America, yet it was a chance to reforge and renew contacts. And my interest in particular was piqued when I learned that the visitor was a young woman and that her mother was Sri Lankan and her father Italian.

It seemed like a sign.

When she arrived, she seemed like a vision.

When she left, I determined to go to America.

I was going to seek a wife.

I was going to meet the Shaykh.

* * *

The shock I'd experienced when seeing the return address on my letter from Frithjof Schuon was no less than the shock felt by the small community of his followers that had already formed in Bloomington, Indiana, when the Shaykh announced he was moving there permanently. Schuon had already visited America a couple of times and been strongly impressed by the rites and beliefs of the Native Americans, and in particular the Oglala Sioux. For Schuon, the Sun Dance, and the very faces and bearing of some of the Native Americans he met, were glimpses into a primordial past when men were closer to God, seeing by direct, symbolic intuition what we could only appreciate now through laborious thought.

But it was still a big thing for a seventy-three-year-old man to up sticks and move continents. It was an even bigger thing for a community that had always been on the margins, set in a little university town that hardly anyone had ever heard of, to have such a man coming to live among them. A tariqa had formed in Bloomington in 1967 around the nucleus of Victor Danner, a professor of religious studies at Indiana University. Frithjof Schuon moved into a house on the outskirts of Bloomington, with other members of the order living in the surrounding buildings.

And that's when things started to go wrong.

In his memoirs, Schuon writes how he sought signs from God when faced with an intractable dilemma. When wrestling with the question of whether he should embrace Islam, he went out into the street after praying for a sign, to see a procession of North African drummers, something that was far from usual at the time, and took this as God's answer. His move to Bloomington was also, apparently, in response to a further sign.

For, as with Blake, Schuon's life was lit by visions. One, in 1973, brought with it "the overwhelming consciousness that I am not as other men".[93] The awestruck disciples in America very much agreed.

---

93   Sedgwick, 2004, page 170.

***

"You know about the Shaykh's wife?"

I was shortly to leave for Bloomington, a flight in late November when the air fares were at their lowest, and I was speaking to one of my friends from the tariqa. He was the first of us younger men to have visited Bloomington, having gone there a few months previously; we'd all quizzed him about it and he'd been enthusiastic but guarded.

"Yes," I said. "I'm going to meet her and then the Shaykh himself."

"It was a white wedding – you know that?"

Thinking all weddings were back then, I must have looked blank.

"It was a vision. The marriage was to be… pure."

I looked at him. "You mean?"

My friend nodded. "Yes."

"Well, sure." I must still have looked puzzled. Why was he telling me this?

My friend cleared his throat. "You've seen pictures of the Shaykh? You can see, he's a passionate man with a virile nature."

I nodded. I had seen one or two photographs of Frithjof Schuon; he did not look the sort of man for whom celibacy came easy, but hearing this of him, I respected his self-control the more.

"Um, as you know, in Islamic law a man may have more than one wife. The Shaykh married again."

I looked at him.

"While keeping his first wife? The one he has a 'white marriage' with?"

My friend was, I thought, showing signs of blushing. He nodded.

I pursed my lips, shrugged. After all, the Shaykh had lived a celibate, married life for many years. Some relief might be in order.

"He has four wives now."

I stared at my friend. "What?"

"Four. He has four wives. As allowed in Islamic law."

I stared, open-mouthed.

"At least he doesn't have any concubines…"

* * *

In Bloomington, Schuon instituted "Indian Days" along with the regular weekly meetings for prayer and the remembrance of God that were the core practice of the order in the rest of the world.

Schuon and his wife – his first wife – had been adopted into the Sioux nation when they had first visited America in 1959, and they had returned for further, long visits before moving permanently to the States. They had attended a Sun Dance on that first visit. The Sun Dance is the great rite of the Oglala Sioux, when a sacred tree is erected and, during the three or four days of the ceremony, expiation and sacrifice are offered.

Indian Days were not Sun Dances but, I was told before going, an effort to anchor the physical recreation of the community in Bloomington in something more sacred than games of basketball. As such, they featured dancing, drumming, and singing. And, yes, I was going to have to wear a loincloth.

There are some sticking points that ride on a great point of principle, and others that come from a slow accumulation of misgivings, but too little cognizance has been given before now on the importance of sheer embarrassment in the rising up and saying, "No."

I had worn a loincloth once before. When I was fourteen and playing a non-speaking Indian in the school production of Bertolt Brecht's play *Buffalo Bill and the Indians*. What I had to do was dance the Sun Dance, while wearing a loincloth, around a sacred tree (which had to be imaginary as we didn't have the props to provide one) and pretending to have hooks piercing my chest muscles, ripping the flesh from me. As far as the audience could see, we were stumbling around in a circle, looking as if we were all subject to dreadfully painful cases of intestinal bloating, before falling to the ground. While wearing loincloths.

Damn it, I was wearing trousers.

They had them: buckskin trousers, like you see in Western films, and as I put them on in that changing room I looked around. Men, middle-aged mostly, but some old and some young, were getting changed around me and all of us, despite the best efforts of exercise and diet, bore the marks of the comfortable, well-fed life of the modern Westerner. And we were putting on loincloths, buckskin shirts, headdresses. I was, at least, safe in my trousers.

The drum started and we filed out and lined up. The room was big, huge really. Some of these people in Bloomington had mansions rather than houses, and I was in the basement of one of them: a room easily large enough to hold a banquet in.

Then the women entered. Most wore buckskin dresses but some of the younger women had on what could only be described as buckskin bikinis; but then, alongside me, were men dressed only in loincloth and beads.

The drums sounded, pounding rhythm – I was about to see the man I had crossed an ocean for – and Frithjof Schuon entered the room. If any elderly white European could carry off being dressed as a Native American chief with full headdress, he was the one.

* * *

Signs are dangerous things. I had crossed the ocean to seek a wife and, a few days into my visit, I was standing beside her, standing as if on the water itself in the middle of a lake. Above us, the moon shone in a clear sky, encircled by a halo spreading the colours of the spectrum into the night, when a shooting star plunged to the moon.

Surely that was a sign of God's favour, of a love sanctioned by heaven and a marriage destined by Providence. Turned out it wasn't even the sign of a short fling.

Like I said, signs are dangerous things. Sometimes they work, sometimes they don't. A few years later, when I first became engaged to the woman I would marry, I had a serious case of nerves and cold feet, and thought of calling the marriage off, only to dream that night that I had won the National Lottery and then thrown away the ticket. I have never before, or since, had a significant dream, but that dream was a true sign.

I had not realized before how appallingly difficult it must be to live amid signs and visions. It was what I had wanted when I set out on this quest: to see, directly. William Blake had lived with visions throughout his life, but his great blessing was to be thought mad, and thus have no followers, no disciples, heaping their weight of expectation and hope upon him. Frithjof Schuon lived with visions throughout his life, and followers gathered around him, and covered him with dreams.

On the regular Sunday afternoon walks I took with Martin Lings I saw him walk, one after another, with people who placed the burdens of their lives on his thin shoulders, and he bore the weight without flinching.

In Bloomington, I saw the weight of dreams, and it was beyond bearing.

* * *

I went into the Shaykh's presence. I sat with Frithjof Schuon for a few minutes, mainly in silence. I sat with a genius, a poet, a philosopher, a man who might have shaken worlds and broken kingdoms. I sat with a good man, who told me to pray. I sat with a man burdened with dreams.

* * *

I came home, to London. And I left the tariqa.

Oh, the leaving was long. A gradual tapering away. But after Martin Lings died in 2005 there was nothing further to keep me.

I had seen, at first hand, the unique possibilities and perils of religious genius. That Frithjof Schuon was a religious genius I had no doubt. Of the extraordinary difficulties attendant on that sort of genius I now also had first-hand knowledge.

And I began to see patterns to this genius, recurring through history.

The great historian Christopher Dawson noted how religions don't so much arise from civilizations as create them:

> The great civilizations of the world do not produce the great
> religions as a kind of cultural by-product; in a very real sense,
> the great religions are the foundations on which the great
> civilizations rest. A society which has lost its religion becomes
> sooner or later a society which has lost its culture.[94]

How often had a religious genius, gathering followers about him, gone into exile as a result of signs and visions, there gathering his strength – and, usually it seemed, wives – before his vindication? Thus had Frithjof Schuon done, and before him Joseph Smith, the founder of the Mormons. Martin Luther, another German, had had similar crises and lived a life patterned on the same template. And,

---

94 Dawson, 2001, page 180.

most tellingly, the man whose example I now ostensibly followed, the Prophet Muhammad, had lived this pattern as well.

In Bloomington, I found myself in a cult centred upon a man who had not the strength or, in the end, the inclination to lift the weight of dreams from his shoulder. By the last few years of his life, the speculation was openly made, not "Who is the Shaykh?" but "What is the Shaykh?", with disciples vying with each other in a religious rank race, seeking always to push him higher and higher: spiritual master, spiritual pole (*qutb*), *pneumatikos*, avatar.

Worship bends men, it breaks them. I don't believe it broke Frithjof Schuon, but it bent him. And with his bending, all that he wrote and taught is called into question.

Much of it is valid.

The rigour of his and Guénon's attack on modern culture will, I hope, help give the Muslim world the intellectual self-confidence to withstand the worst aspects of the West and thus, finally, outgrow the corrosive lack of self-belief that has led to the gun and the bomb being chosen as the method of counter-attack.

His insight into spiritual states and moods, and the meaning of sacred art, is extraordinary.

But the message, in its entirety, stood upon it being realized in the person who most espoused it. In that, Frithjof Schuon failed, and the message fails with him.

* * *

Let's be honest here: I was pretty rubbish at the methods of prayer practised by the tariqa. Sitting cross-legged, invoking the Divine Name, sent me to sleep more effectively than a cup of cocoa. The themes of meditation that were supposed to lead down into the Divine Nature infallibly drew me down into daydream. Maybe, if I'd been better at all this, if God had seen me nodding off, my head doing the pigeon peck of the sleep fighter, and decided to shock me into attention by removing his veils, then I would still be in the tariqa. After all, it was a principle of its method that turning to God necessarily made him turn towards us: "It is in trusting to that [teachings and method] that we 'obligate' God toward us."[95] So, if I had just kept going and closed my mind to doubts, then maybe I would have seen, and known it all to be true. It is possible – but it could only have happened if I had turned away from further knowledge.

I returned to London, to the city that had given birth to the modern world so excoriated by the Traditionalist writers, and set about resuming my life.

It was time to learn, to see if the central claims made by the Perennialists, the claims that I had accepted, really held up. While the messenger had failed, maybe his message was still valid.

I enrolled on an MA in religion and discovered that no, the claims did not hold up. Only by making an *a priori* assumption of the truth of the amalgam of Advaita Vedanta and Neoplatonism employed by Traditionalist writers to view the world's religions could aspects of those religions be turned into pages from the same book. Only by ignoring key aspects of those religions and, in the case of Theravada Buddhism, the religion itself, could the religions be squeezed into the same box. Only by begging the question of the validity of the intellectual intuition so adverted in their writings could the Perennialists avoid the hard questions of demonstrations of intuited truth: you either "saw" it – in which case you were qualified for the truth; or you didn't – in which case you weren't capable of the truth.

This was truth reserved for an elite.

The problem was, we weren't much of an elite.

---

95 Sedgwick, 2004, page 153.

Some were. I have met no finer, or holier, man than Martin Lings, although I have known some his equal in other contexts and different countries. But the truth or otherwise of the Perennialist claims – many of which are not demonstrable to scholarship but depend upon the sort of "aha" moment of recognition that Martin Lings experienced when he first read René Guénon – then requires further support in their effects: do those who talk this talk, walk it too?

As I said, religious genius is the greatest burden and heaviest temptation that can be laid upon a human being: is it so surprising that it breaks those upon whom it is placed? I have no animus towards Frithjof Schuon – I pray for the repose of his soul every night – but the fond old belief that God does not test people beyond their strength is just not true; some he breaks by taking, others he breaks by giving. God is a fire. He devours. He burns.

> You can run on for a long time
> Run on for a long time
> Run on for a long time
> Sooner or later God'll cut you down. (Traditional)

And those who constrain him in words, he chops off at the knees. St Thomas Aquinas was reduced to silence in the final few months of his life, after he saw that all he had written was as straw before the reality. Metaphysics is a compulsive pursuit, but philosophers and theologians beware, for there is one thing we do know about God: he tells stories – and a good story will not be constrained.

CHAPTER 9

CITY OF GOD

I pace the pavements, treading prayer into stone.

There was a lot of that, then. Walking, through the parks and streets of London. The best time to walk is early, before the sun has risen but when the sky is lightening: dawn. Then the city is quiet and even the people who are professionally up at this time go about with the calm that comes of moving in the midst of sleeping multitudes. You can almost hear the city's breath: low, slow, then quickening as the rhythm builds to waking.

There is a church in the heart of Soho, Soho Square to be precise, that presents a thin, red-brick face to the world, rising in narrow frontage to its bell tower. I was working near there, walking out for early lunch, when I heard it toll the Angelus – three rings, a pause, three again, pause once more, then a final three – and I went to find the church. Outside, narrow, slightly forbidding. Inside, opening out hugely, so it seemed a Tardis church – how could something so expansive appear so small from without?

Along one wall, three of the old-fashioned wooden cubicles used for confession. In my local parish church, these had been done away with in favour of face-to-face encounters with the priest; I was not ready for that.

A stole hung from the confessional. A priest sat ready within.

I knelt.

Through the grill, I could discern his shadow silhouette, head bowed. Without turning his head he placed us under the blessing. "In the name of the Father, the Son, and the Holy Spirit. Amen."

"Bless me, Father, for I have sinned." I paused. "I… I can't remember how long it's been since my last confession…"

And, when it was over, when I'd stumbled through my words, and the priest had asked of me what seemed a most meagre penance – surely I ought to do more than a few prayers? – he began to pronounce the formula of absolution.

"God, the Father of mercies, through the death and resurrection of his Son has reconciled the world to himself and sent the Holy Spirit among us for the forgiveness of sins; through the ministry of the Church may God give you pardon and peace…"

As he spoke the words, the memory of my eight-year-old self returned, waiting for the revelation that never came when I received Holy Communion for the first time.

"… and I, an unworthy priest, absolve you from your sins in the name of the Father, and of the Son, and of the Holy Spirit."

I was here, but I did not really know why. In the end, I had returned to where I had begun.

And as the priest spoke those final words, I felt as if a band I had not known was there, slowly tightening through the years around my chest, had let go; I had been chained, and not known it. I had been bound, and now I was free.

I said those few, small prayers, and knew.

There was nothing earned in that forgiveness. It was nothing to do with my prayers and invocations and meditations; with my reading and thinking and doing.

It was a gift.

Later, after I had taken to hearing lunchtime Mass whenever I was working in central London, I learned that St Patrick's, Soho, was where my parents had married in 1962.

The church itself lies on the site of Carlisle House, where one of Casanova's mistresses, Teresa Cornelys, lived, holding soirées, masquerades, and balls to which all the most fashionable members of society came. Cornelys lived with a flamboyance to match the entertainments she oversaw, continually falling into debt and almost as frequently into debtors' prison. Just across from the square was the Rookery at St Giles, one of the most notorious slums in London and home to thousands of impoverished Irish; with the penal anti-Catholic laws, there was no church to minister to them until the passing of the Catholic Relief Act of 1791. In response "'a very numerous and respectable body of Catholics conceived the wise and Charitable project of establishing a Catholic Chapel' in the neighbourhood of St. Giles's, which was 'inhabited principally by the poorest and least informed of the Irish who resort to this Country'".[96] The present building was finished in 1893.

Immigrants bring their gods with them. My father arrived in 1960. He came by boat, sailing from Colombo, across the Indian Ocean and through the Suez Canal, before entering the calm waters of the Mediterranean and then the decidedly less calm waters of the Atlantic. He arrived in winter and, at first, he thought some dreadful blight had fallen upon this new country, for all the trees were dead.

During World War II, my father and his brother enlisted in the army. Ceylonese (as they were still, then), brown-skinned sons of the Empire, they fought for it, even though Uncle Andrew had been vehement in his calls for Ceylon's independence. Father served in Ceylon, manning anti-aircraft guns in Trincomalee, but Uncle Andrew fought with the Eighth Army, advancing and retreating and advancing again through the countries of North

---

96   Sheppard, 1966a, page 79.

Africa. I have a photo of him, in military fatigues, but with a keffiyeh over his head.

The British Nationality Act of 1948 gave right of abode in Britain to any subjects of the Empire. Uncle Andrew's commanding officer offered to help him settle in Britain after the war, but he decided to stay in Ceylon as it moved towards independence. My father stayed as well, but as work became harder to find in post-independence Sri Lanka, he started to look abroad and, in 1960, he caught the boat.

He was not alone. Speak to older people. Then, it was possible to walk out of one job in the morning and start another in the afternoon, employers were so desperate to fill vacancies. Indeed, such was their desperation that they started advertising for brown- and black-skinned people to come over and take these jobs.

Do I sympathize with the people who decided to slam the door in the faces of the people who had been invited? Actually, I do. It is no easy matter to see a neighbourhood one has known since childhood transformed, and while some might welcome the change, others will not: this is not a matter of morality but the tension between the desire for novelty and the wish for stability that contends, unevenly, in everyone.

The response was the Commonwealth Immigrants Act of 1962. It didn't slam the door, but it began to push it closed, at least against the feared wave of dark-skinned people. As the Home Secretary, Rab Butler, said in the debate on the Act:

> We all know that throughout the continuous evolution of the Commonwealth, citizens of member-States have always been free to come here and stay here as long as they like. This has been a cherished tradition of the Mother Country and there is little doubt that it has been an important link binding the Commonwealth together....

The justification for the control which is included in this Bill... is that a sizeable part of the entire population of the earth is at present legally entitled to come and stay in this already densely populated country. It amounts altogether to one-quarter of the population of the globe and at present there are no factors visible which might lead us to expect a reversal or even a modification of the immigration trend which I am about to describe.[97]

Father made it to the Mother Country just in time.

Italians, on the other hand, had been in London for centuries. Lombard Street was named after the bankers from Lombardia who lived there and there was a continuing Italian presence through the centuries. Shakespeare set a third of his plays in Italy and a contemporary, John Florio, taught Italian to the eldest son of James I (Prince Henry died at eighteen, leaving the accession to his younger brother, Charles – just one of many historical what ifs). But the first real wave of Italian immigration followed in the wake of the Napoleonic wars. The conflict had passed backwards and forwards through northern Italy, devastating farms and livelihoods. In response, Italians started walking. Men would tramp across the mountain passes, into France and on through the long trudge northwards, setting off in the spring and returning before winter, taking what work they could find in England, and particularly London. The first immigrants were from Como and Lucca, but these were succeeded in the 1870s by men from Parma, mainly organ grinders, and the Liri valley, who were ice-cream makers.

Many of these first Italians lived in Clerkenwell and, with Catholic emancipation, they brought their God: St Peter's Italian Church was consecrated on 16 April 1863. It still stands, all white marble

---

97 Source: http://hansard.millbanksystems.com/commons/1961/nov/16/commonwealth-immigrants-bill#S5CV0649P0_19611116_HOC_285.

and madonnas, and one Sunday every July Italians return from the suburbs to which they've largely moved and process around the streets, with floats displaying religious tableaux in honour of Our Lady of Mount Carmel. The food's pretty good too.

All those poor Italians opened coffee bars and restaurants in Soho and Covent Garden and, with some money made, promptly moved to the suburbs, leaving Clerkenwell to the hipsters. Something like a third of the houses in the streets immediately around me must belong to Italians – they (we) like to huddle together, and to take packs of Lavazza when venturing abroad.

It's different for Sri Lankans. Those who came, like my father, to better themselves in the 1950s and 1960s largely did so, following the core Asian path: hard work in the first generation and hard study in the second. It was more difficult for those who came in the 1980s and 1990s, since many arrived as refugees from the civil war in Sri Lanka. The ethnic tensions that had resulted in war at home largely fractured the amity that had previously existed between expat Sinhalese and Tamils; now they live in parallel communities, rarely touching each other.

Although my father is Christian, the majority of Sinhalese are Buddhists, while most Tamils are Hindu. When I was at a low ebb – all right, my parents thought I was suicidal – my Uncle Wijeratne (not actually an uncle, but you call everyone Uncle, Auntie, or Cousin) brought a monk from the Chiswick Temple, the London Buddhist Vihara, to chant for me. I was so embarrassed I promptly rose from my depression-induced dullness before he even cleared his throat – so it worked. Nowadays, mindfulness meditative techniques derived from Buddhist practices have become important treatments for depression but I submit that a good dose of teenage embarrassment works faster.

The London Buddhist Vihara was established in 1926 as the first Sri Lankan Buddhist monastery outside Asia, starting in

Gloucester Road before moving to Chiswick: first Heathfield Gardens and now The Avenue. A visit for the Vesak celebrations on the full moon of May, when the Buddha's birth, enlightenment, and Parinirvana (passing into Nirvana) are celebrated, is memorable for the garlanded gold statues of the Lord Buddha and the mix of matter-of-fact Sinhalese and earnest Western converts. In the 1990s there was much talk of Buddhism's advance in the West and a number of high-profile conversions (the best known of these was the Italian footballer Roberto Baggio). Many of my friends became interested in Buddhism and started attending talks and meditation sessions, thinking to find the ancient serenity of the East. To further his knowledge of Buddhism, one of my friends decided to come out to join me in Sri Lanka when I spent a few months there in the early 1990s. I still remember his slowly growing shock on the trip back from the airport as the serene and mystic East hit him full force with all five senses and some he hadn't even suspected he had.

The 2011 census recorded 82,026 Buddhists in London, 34 per cent of the Buddhist population of England. In comparison, for London the census found 3,957,984 Christians, 411,291 Hindus, 148,602 Jews, 1,012,823 Muslims, 126,134 Sikhs, 47,970 people of other religions, and 1,694,372 of no religion.

It's impossible to give an accurate figure for the number of Sri Lankans or people of Sri Lankan descent in the UK as the government lumps us all together as South Asian – an even broader generalization than lumping all Europeans together. If I was inclined towards taking offence, I probably would.

Instead, I attend my local parish church on Sunday. It was built in the 1930s; it's no architectural marvel – the architect's original ambitious plan was cut off halfway through when funds ran out and the builders, building from the altar and chancel outwards, simply ended the church where they'd got to, losing the planned basilica-style entrance and bell tower – but at least it doesn't set out to actively sabotage prayer and undermine worship, unlike some modern churches. I've even grown fond of the huge statue of the Risen Christ that the previous parish priest commissioned and had installed in the chancel – the hair, spreading like that of the best professional shampoo model from his scalp, apparently represents Christ rising from hell upon the breath of the Holy Spirit.

It's an ordinary north London parish served by priests who don't claim to be anything other than priests. The congregation is... well, people. The mix, running through all social classes and ethnic groups, is what you find in churches. It's no elite organization, there are no secret teachings and, really, it's pretty ordinary. But I meet God there. I meet him whenever I go to Mass, in the silence of sacraments, beyond words, in the real, physical presence of this world and the next: bread, wine, water.

I began this book beneath the belly of a whale. I will end it by walking, pacing prayer into the stones of this city of God. My life has been one of small compass, lived up and down the Piccadilly Line. I will walk from the centre to my home, from St Patrick's in Soho to Our Lady of Lourdes in the suburbs, looking to see the signs of God in the city of the world.

***

Well, that was pretty gruelling. Not the walking, although twelve miles on hard pavements was enough to leave muscles aching and a knee sore. No, it was the ghosts. I didn't expect them. But they swarmed around me, moths of memory, flapping across my sight and through my mind. The boy I was, the boys I knew; they walked with me although they are all dead.

This is, I see now, a city of ghosts. We, the living, are less substantial than they; we drift through them.

It was as well that the old Foyles is closed now, awaiting the redevelopment that is washing through the whole area around Tottenham Court Road Tube station in anticipation of Crossrail; if it had been open, or accessible, the whispering, the murmur of all those books would have held me tighter than memory.

Books have ghosts too, you know. Curiously, these ghosts are not particularly apparent in the second-hand bookshops on and off the Charing Cross Road; in these shops, the books wait in expectation. But go to a charity shop or, even more so, a restaurant or hotel that has bought books by the yard to fill shelves and then you will feel the ghosts, as words and stories coil in upon themselves.

From Leicester Square, I walked past the bookshops, sometimes touching a spine or a jacket with a trailing finger for the feel of paper and the benediction of words: remember, books were my first church and here there are many chapels. I went to Foyles, the new Foyles: light and airy and spacious – as far from the cramped and crabbed space of old as is possible within the confines of still having lots of books on shelves. A fine bookshop, I suppose, and they do have my books for sale, but too much like everywhere else.

On the corner of Soho Square is the House of St Barnabas. Once a hostel for the homeless, it was founded in 1846 "for the relief of the destitute and the houseless poor in London". Its two principal objects were "to afford temporary relief to as many destitute cases as possible, and to have a Christian effect on the poor population,[98]" and William Gladstone was among its sponsors. It continued its charitable work throughout the twentieth century, at one time providing beds for 800 women, but the hostel closed in 2006. And it became a private-members' club. A supremely trendy private-members' club, with founders

---

98 Sheppard, 1966b.

including Jarvis Cocker and Gilles Peterson, it allows all the networking creatives to feel really good about themselves by using part of their subscription to fund its employment and skills programme for the homeless and unemployed. Walk past any lunchtime and, if you stand near the old pipe chute that allowed passers-by to make anonymous coin donations, you'll be almost overwhelmed by the smell of roasting lamb.

That's modern charity for you: doing good while eating well. (My relatives in Sri Lanka, in the aftermath of the tsunami, all noted how the NGOs first secured the best hotels in the island before moving on to disaster relief. After all, why should a commitment to change be linked to personal poverty?)

St Patrick's was a relief. Fr Alexander Sherbrooke, the parish priest, has overseen the church's transformation: not only has he masterminded the renewal and renovation of its interior, but he has founded a school for evangelization, leading young people out onto the streets of Soho to spread, through speech and procession and prayer, the news of hope. After all, what more does Soho (or, indeed, twenty-first-century Western culture in general) offer than an unusually wide range of people with whom to have sex, and the newest iPhone? In such a world, hope is not a luxury, it's an escape.

The Radha Krishna temple of ISKCON (International Society for Krishna Consciousness) is around the corner. Earnest devotees will sometimes press books on me by their founder, Bhaktivedanta Swami Prabhupada, and they regularly bring great juggernauts of the gods out onto the street, flower-garlanded and vivid with chant. It's as if the sound paints the figure with light, however dull the day.

When I worked on the TVs, delivering and repairing televisions and videos and driving round London every day, I'd be up and down, up and down the North Circular as the boxed retail corporations set up warehouses along its length: Tesco, Toys R Us, Ikea. We'd turn off the North Circular at the Ikea junction if we had jobs in Harlesden or Neasden and that's how I got to see the building of the Neasden Temple, or BAPS Shri Swaminaryan Mandir to give it its official title. Much as I love London's suburbs – roll on the day when a row of 1930s semi-detached houses with their front gardens as yet untarmacked is given Grade II protection – even I have to admit that the North Circular spread something of a grey blight around its circuit. That is, until 1992, when volunteers started building the temple from white marble that had first been shipped to India to be carved and then brought to England for assembly. It took two and a half years to build, a progress so quick that it only added to the dream-like nature of the building. Even today, although the early blinding white of the marble has been streaked by twenty years of London rain, the temple still appears as a vision on Brentfield Road.

At the bottom of Tottenham Court Road is the Dominion Theatre. I saw Dexys Midnight Runners play there in 1985, with Kevin Rowland doing push-ups on stage to the apparent bemusement of his bandmates. The theatre was home to the Queen musical, *We Will Rock You*, between 2002 and 2014. When Freddie Mercury died, I saw some footage of his funeral and in among the preening mourners of the rock and entertainment worlds were two diminutive Indian figures, traditionally clad: Mercury's mother and father. They were Parsis and it was a Zoroastrian funeral.

Since 2005, the Dominion has hosted the Sunday services of Hillsong Church, the London branch of the Sydney megachurch. And it is mega. There are four services each Sunday, filling out the theatre. When I went, and spoke to some of the people attending, it was remarkable how much their lives had been transformed by faith. "Church is everything" was a typical response to my question, "What is church?"

But what was remarkable for me was the complete lack of traditional Christian iconography. This was Christianity reimagined for people who wouldn't be seen dead in an ordinary church, and it was working. The place was packed.

London is lonely. I'm not the first and I won't be the last to remark on this or to know this. The ghosts had reminded me of the deep loneliness of the past. But at Hillsong, after the worship music – rather loud and lacking in polyphony for my taste, but well done – everyone in the congregation/audience was enjoined to turn and talk to the people around them; to talk to the people they did not know. Barriers were broken, conversations entered, and lonely people engaged. Then the minister came on stage. His name was Pete Wilson and I met him later at the Hospital Club (a private-members' club founded by Dave Stewart of the Eurythmics and Paul Allen, co-founder of Microsoft), where he did not look at all out of place among the self-consciously cool media types scrolling through their iPads. Wilson was dressed in a black leather bomber jacket and he proceeded to give a tour de force performance in holding an audience with words, while examining a verse from the Bible – I'm ashamed to say I cannot remember which one – and showing its applicability to people's lives. If I had walked in from the street at one of the crisis points in my life, his exposition would likely have served to give me hope.

I had never understood the appeal of Pentecostalism before, nor how it could have gone from barely existing at the start of the twentieth century to claiming over 250 million followers by the end of that century, but now I began to see some of its appeal.

The key that opens the heart to grace is different for everybody; the stripes the world lays upon us are such that sometimes it becomes impossible for a person to appreciate the truth under its clearest forms. Then God must write crooked, that the person might yet read.

Walking north, my ghosts whispering my way, I passed almost the whole panoply of religious belief today: the Scientologists on Tottenham Court Road; the American International Church further up the road; Camden Town Methodist Church; St Michael's Church, Camden Town; the Greek Orthodox Cathedral of All Saints on Camden Street; Holloway Seventh-Day Adventist Church on the Holloway Road; the Al-Risaalah Mosque on Parkhurst Road; St John the Evangelist Church on the Holloway Road; and, just a bit further up, St Gabriel's of childhood memory, now much improved within (there's not much that can be done with the exterior save tearing it down and building afresh); halfway up the hill, St Joseph's Church; Christ Church, Crouch End; Jubilee Church in the Vue Cinema in Wood Green; Zion Church of Christ Apostolic in Perth Road; the Palmers Green and Southgate Synagogue. If my legs hadn't been pretty tired by the end, I could easily have added the Nanak Darbar North London. This chimes pretty well with my experience: around where I live, it seems almost everyone goes to church, mosque, synagogue, gurdwara, or temple. And this in the Great Wen, the city that first gave the finger to God, secure in its wealth and power. But God sneaks in under the radar. Think on this. Of all the movements of armies and emperors in the centuries of Roman rule over what seemed the whole world, the most significant movement was that of a handful of Jews leaving their homeland. No Roman historian noticed a Jew called Paul tramping their roads, but his journeys, and those of the other apostles, proved of more importance than that of any emperor.

The same is true of London today. The city's movers and makers, the talkers and mediacrities that fill screens and pages with prattle, remain blithely unaware of what is going on around them, so secure are they in their bubbles of influence. For London, seemingly without anyone noticing, has become over the last twenty years the most religious part of Britain. Church attendance has risen from just over 620,000 in 2005 to just over 720,000 in 2012 (when the last comprehensive survey was completed). Even more unexpectedly, the percentage of twenty-something Londoners going to church is almost double that for the rest of England. A further 120,000 people attend midweek church activities, which means that all together over 10 per cent of Londoners attend church weekly. And it's not just congregations: the number of churches is growing as well, with a 67 per cent growth in the number of churches in Inner London between 1979 and 2012, and a 25 per cent increase in Outer London over the same period.

This does not surprise me. Years of driving and walking down streets that our modern media figures would never visit have shown me that churches are opening up all over the place, particularly in the Victorian zone of expansion, but often in new and unexpected places: cinema complexes, disused industrial units, closed-down shops, houses. Seeing this fills me with hope: the early Christians had to make do with such make-do premises; watching this happen again suggests that God, yet again, might be pulling one of his bait-and-switch moves on human expectations. The century that was, yet again, supposed to see his end might yet give unexpected birth to rebirth.

Will the country follow London or London follow the rest of the country? History suggests the former: where London has led, England has generally followed.

As have I. This story began under the belly of a whale. It rambled through history and took an unexpected turn abroad, before returning to where it started. A suburban church, with no great pretensions, and a priest who claimed to be nothing other than a priest, an imperfect man in service of a dangerous God, sitting behind a screen and hearing my confession.

And when I finished and he, "an unworthy priest", said the words of absolution, I felt a band drawn tight around my chest, a chain I had not even known was there, loosen and let go.

I pace the pavements, treading prayer into stone.

BIBLIOGRAPHY

Abels, Richard P., *Lordship and Military Obligation in Anglo-Saxon England*, London: British Museum Publications, 1988.

Abels, Richard, *Alfred the Great: War, Kingship and Culture in Anglo-Saxon England*, London: Routledge, 1998.

Ackroyd, Peter, *Blake*, London: Vintage Books, 1995.

Ackroyd, Peter, *London: The Biography*, London: Vintage Books, 2000.

Ackroyd, Peter, *London Under: the secret history beneath the streets*, London: Vintage Books, 2012.

Adams, Douglas, *The Salmon of Doubt: Hitchhiking the Galaxy One Last Time*, London: Pan, 2012.

Alexander, Michael, *The Earliest English Poems*, Harmondsworth: Penguin, 1977.

Arrian, William Dansey, *Arrian on coursing: the Cynegeticus of the younger Xenophon, translated from the Greek, with classical and practical annotations, and a brief sketch of the life and writings of the author. To which is added an appendix, containing some account of the Canes venatici of classical antiquity*, London: J. Bohn, 1831. https://archive.org/details/arrianoncoursing00arri [Accessed 1 September 2015].

Barber, Bruno, Thomas, Christopher and Watson, Bruce, *Religion in Medieval London: Archaeology and Belief*, London: Museum of London Archaeology, 2013.

Barber, Lynn, *The Heyday of Natural History*, London: Jonathan Cape, 1980.

Bede, *Ecclesiastical History of the English People*. Translated by Leo Sherley-Price, London: Penguin, 1990.

Bentley, G. E., *Blake Records*, Oxford: Oxford University Press, 1969.

Bentley, G. E., *Blake Records Supplement: Being New Materials Relating to the Life of William Blake Discovered Since the Publication of Blake Records (1969)*, Oxford: Oxford University Press, 1988.

Bentley, Gerald Eades and Bentley Jr, G., *William Blake: The Critical Heritage*, London: Routledge, 1995.

Besant, Annie, *An Autobiography*, Project Gutenberg ebook, 2004. http://www.gutenberg.org/files/12085/12085-h/12085-h.htm [Accessed 24 July 2015].

Blair, J., *The Church in Anglo-Saxon Society*, Oxford: Oxford University Press, 2005.

Blair, Peter Hunter, *An Introduction to Anglo-Saxon England*, Cambridge: Cambridge University Press, 1977.

Blake, William, *Poems and Prophecies,* London: Everyman's Library, 1972.

Blake, William, *The Complete Poetry and Prose*, ed. D. V. Erdman, Oakland: University of California Press, 1982.

Blavatsky, Helena, *Collected Writings Online*, vol. XII, nd. http://www.katinkahesselink.net/blavatsky/articles/v12/y1890_052.htm [Accessed 9 November 2015].

Brierley, Peter, *Capital Growth: What the 2012 London Church Census Reveals,* Tonbridge: ADBC Publishers, 2013.

Brigden, Susan, *New Worlds, Lost Worlds: The Rule of the Tudors, 1485–1603*, London: Penguin, 2000.

Brigden, Susan, *London and the Reformation*, London: Faber & Faber, 2014.

Burnet, Gilbert, *The History of the Reformation of the Church of England*, Oxford: Clarendon Press, 1816.

Campbell, James (ed.), *The Anglo-Saxons*, Oxford: Phaidon Press, 1982.

Carpenter, Humphrey, *The Inklings: C.S. Lewis, J.R.R. Tolkien, Charles Williams and their friends*, London: HarperCollins, 1997.

Cavendish, Richard, *Encylopedia of the Unexplained: Magic, Occultism and Parapsychology*, London: Routledge and Kegan Paul, 1974.

Census of Great Britain, 1851, *Religious worship. England and Wales. Report and tables*, House of Commons Parliamentary Papers online, 1851.

Chalmers, Alexander, *The General Biographical Dictionary,* London: J. Nichols, 1815.

Chesterton, G. K., *The Father Brown Stories*, London: Cassell & Company, 1960.

Crawford, Sally, *Daily Life in Anglo-Saxon England*, Oxford: Greenwood World Publishing, 2009.

Dawson, Christopher, *Progress and Religion: An Historical Enquiry*, Washington, DC: Catholic University of America Press, 2001.

Dekker, Thomas, *The Gull's Hornbook*, London: De la More Press, 1905. https://openlibrary.org/books/OL5078166M/The_gull%27s_hornbook [Accessed 4 November 2015].

Dicuil, *Liber de Mensura Orbis Terrae*, nd. http://penelope.uchicago.edu/ Thayer/E/Roman/Texts/Dicuil/De_mensura_orbis_terrae/text*.html [Accessed 1 September 2015].

Duffy, Eamon, *The Stripping of the Altars: Traditional Religion in England c.1400–c.1580*, New Haven, CT: Yale University Press, 1992.

Dunn, Marilyn, *The Christianization of the Anglo-Saxons c.597–c.700: Discourses of Life, Death and Afterlife*, London: Continuum, 2009.

Eliot, T. S., *Collected Poems 1909–1962*, London: Faber & Faber, 1980.

Essick, Robert N., "Blake, William (1757–1827)", *Oxford Dictionary of National Biography*, Oxford: Oxford University Press, 2004; online edn, Oct 2005. http://www.oxforddnb.com/view/article/2585 [Accessed 20 August 2015].

Fraser, Antonia, *The Six Wives of Henry VIII,* London: Phoenix Press, 2007.

Gething, Paul and Albert, Edoardo, *Northumbria: The Lost Kingdom*, Stroud: The History Press, 2012.

Gilchrist, Alexander, *The Life of William Blake*, London: John Lane the Bodley Head, 1907. https://archive.org/stream/lifewilliamblak01 gilcgoog#page/n12/mode/2up [Accessed 2 September 2015].

Girouard, Mark, *Alfred Waterhouse and the Natural History Museum*, New Haven, CT: Yale University Press, 1981.

Hansard, HC Deb 16 November 1961, vol. 649, cc687–819.

Hendriks, Lawrence, *The London Charterhouse: Its Monks and Its Martyrs*, London: Kegan Paul, Trench & Co, 1889.

Hendriks, Lawrence, *The Carthusian Martyrs*, London: Catholic Truth Society, 1928.

Higham, N. J., *The Kingdom of Northumbria AD 350–1100,* Dover: Allan Sutton, 1993.

Hughes, Pennethorne, *Witchcraft*, Harmondsworth: Penguin, 1965.

Hunting, Penelope, *Royal Westminster: A History of Westminster through its Royal Connections*, London: Royal Institution of Chartered Surveyors, 1981.

Huxley, T. H., *Life and Letters of Thomas Henry Huxley,* vol. 1, ed. Leonard Huxley, Cambridge: Cambridge University Press, 1903.

Ingram, James (trans.), *The Anglo-Saxon Chronicle*, London: Everyman, 1912. http://www.britannia.com/history/docs/asintro2.html [Accessed 2 September 2015].

Inwood, Stephen, *A History of London*, London: Macmillan, 1998.

Jacobs, Joseph, *The Jews of Angevin England: Documents and Records, from the Latin and Hebrew Sources*, London: G.P. Putnam, 1893. https://openlibrary.org/books/OL6952272M/The_Jews_of_Angevin_England [Accessed 20 March 2015].

Johnson, Boris, *Johnson's Life of London: The People Who Made the City That Made the World*, London: HarperCollins, 2012.

Johnston, William, *Silent Music: The Science of Meditation*, London: William Collins, 1974.

Jones, F. L. (ed.), *The Letters of Percy Bysshe Shelley*, Oxford: Oxford University Press, 1964.

Keynes, Geoffrey (ed.), *Letters of William Blake*, Cambridge, MA: Harvard University Press, 1970.

Keynes, Simon and Lapidge, Michael (translators), *Alfred the Great: Asser's Life of King Alfred and Other Contemporary Sources*, London: Penguin, 2004.

Langland, William, *The Book Concerning Piers the Plowman*. Translated by Donald and Rachel Attwater, London: Everyman, 1957.

Latham, Martin, *Londonopolis: A Curious History of London*, London: Batsford, 2014.

Lewis, C. S., *Essays Presented to Charles Williams*, Grand Rapids, MI: William B. Eerdmans, 1966.

Lewis, C. S., *English Literature in the Sixteenth Century, Excluding Drama*, Oxford: Oxford University Press, 1973.

Lewis, C. S., *The Silver Chair*, Harmondsworth: Puffin, 1976.

Lings, Martin, "Frithjof Schuon: An Autobiographical Approach", *Sophia*, 1998, 4/2, 15–16.

Magee, Bryan, *Men of Ideas: Some Creators of Contemporary Philosophy*, New York: Viking Press, 1978.

Marlowe, Christopher, *The Complete Plays*, Harmondsworth: Penguin, 1969.

Marsh, Christopher, *Religion and the State in Russia and China: Suppression, Survival, and Revival*, London: Continuum, 2011.

Mayr-Harting, Henry, *The Coming of Christianity to Anglo-Saxon England*, London: B.T. Batsford, 1991.

Merton, Thomas, *The Silent Life*, New York: Farrar, Straus and Giroux, 1957. http://transfiguration.chartreux.org/Merton-on-Carthusians.htm [Accessed 1 September 2015].

Milman, Henry Hart, *Annals of St. Paul's Cathedral*, London: John Murray, 1868. https://openlibrary.org/books/OL20449284M/Annals_of_St._Paul's_Cathedral [Accessed 9 March 2015].

Moorman, John R. H., *A History of the Church in England*, London: Adam and Charles Black, 1958.

Oxford Concise Dictionary of Quotations, Oxford: Oxford University Press, 2011.

Peddie, John, *Alfred the Good Soldier: His Life & Campaigns*, Bath: Millstream Books, 1992.

Pierce, Patricia, *Old London Bridge: The Story of the Longest Inhabited Bridge in Europe*, London: Headline Books, 2001.

Pollard, Justin, *Alfred the Great: The Man who Made England*, London: John Murray, 2006.

Richards, J. D., "Pagans and Christians at the Frontier: Viking Burial in the Danelaw", in Carver, M. O. H. (ed.), *The Cross Goes North: Processes of Conversion in Northern Europe, AD 300–1300*, York/Woodbridge: York Medieval Press in association with Boydell & Brewer, 2003, pp. 383–95. http://eprints.whiterose.ac.uk/archive/00000755/ [Accessed: 10 February 2015].

Rogers, Ben, *A.J. Ayer: A Life*, London: Chatto & Windus, 1999.

Royal Irish Academy, *The Cathach/The Psalter of St Columba*, 2015. http://www.ria.ie/Library/Special-Collections/Manuscripts/Cathach.aspx [Accessed 1 September 2015].

Schofield, John, "Saxon London in a Tale of Two Cities", *British Archaeology*, 1999, 44.

Sedgwick, Mark, *Against the Modern World: Traditionalism and the Secret Intellectual History of the Twentieth Century*, Oxford: Oxford University Press, 2004.

Sheppard, F. H. W. (ed.), "Soho Square Area: Portland Estate, St. Patrick's Roman Catholic Church and Presbytery, Soho Square", in *Survey of London: Volumes 33 and 34, St Anne Soho*, London: London County Council, 1966a, pp. 79–81. http://www.british-history.ac.uk/survey-london/vols33-4/pp79-81 [Accessed 26 August 2015].

Sheppard, F. H. W. (ed.), "Soho Square Area: Portland Estate: No. 1 Greek Street: The House of St. Barnabas-in-Soho", in *Survey of London: Volumes 33 and 34, St Anne Soho*, London: London County Council, 1966b, pp. 88–106. http://www.british-history.ac.uk/survey-london/vols33-4/pp88-106 [Accessed 29 August 2015].

Spencer, Nick, *Atheists: The Origin of the Species*, London: Bloomsbury, 2014.

Sponza, Lucio, *Italian Immigrants in Nineteenth-Century Britain: Reality and Images*, Leicester: Leicester University Press, 1988.

Spurgeon, Caroline F. E., *Mysticism in English Literature. Project Gutenberg*, 2004. http://www.gutenberg.org/files/11935/11935-h/11935-h.htm [Accessed 20 August 2015].

Stow, John, "Sports and Pastimes of Old Time", in *A Survey of London. Reprinted From the Text of 1603*, ed. C. L. Kingsford, Oxford: Clarendon, 1908, pp. 91–99. http://www.british-history.ac.uk/no-series/survey-of-london-stow/1603/pp91-99 [Accessed 13 February 2015].

Tacitus, *Annals of Imperial Rome*. Translated by Michael Grant, Harmondsworth: Penguin, 1956.

Tolkien, J. R. R., *The Silmarillion*, London: George Allen & Unwin, 1977.

Webb, Beatrice, *My Apprenticeship*, Cambridge: Cambridge University Press, 1979.

Weightman, Gavin, *London's Thames*, London: John Murray, 2004.

Whitelock, Dorothy, *English Historical Documents: Volume 1, c.500–1042*, London: Eyre & Spottiswode, 1979.

Williams, Charles, *All Hallows' Eve*, Grand Rapids, MI: William Eerdmans, 1991.

Williams, Charles, *War in Heaven*, Grand Rapids, MI: William Eerdmans, 1994.

Wilson, A. N., *London: A Short History*, London: Phoenix, 2005.

Yeats, W. B., *The Collected Letters of W.B. Yeats: Volume 1: 1865–1895,* ed. John Kelly and Eric Domville, Oxford: Clarendon Press, 1986.

If you love EDOARDO ALBERT's writing,
don't miss out on his fiction…

EDWIN: HIGH KING OF BRITAIN

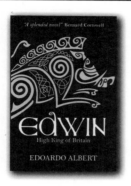

"A splendid novel"
BERNARD CORNWELL

Edwin is a king. Yet he is about to be betrayed
and butchered.

Edwin, the long-exiled king of Northumbria, thought he had found
sanctuary at the court of King Rædwald – his friend, and now
protector.

But Rædwald faces the lure of riches and the threat of bloodshed,
and Edwin fears that he will be abandoned to his enemies.

As Edwin contemplates his fate, a mysterious messenger prophesies
that he will ascend to greater heights than any of his forefathers.

Can Edwin escape the fearsome warrior king who is calling for
his blood? Do the Anglo-Saxon Gods of old, or the new God
from across the sea, really have the power to raise Edwin above
all other kings?

ISBN: 978-1-78264-033-2 | e-ISBN: 978-1-78264-061-5

UK £7.99 | US $14.99